Under a Canvas Sky

Under a Canvas Sky

Clare Peake

CONSTABLE • LONDON

Constable & Robinson Ltd
3 The Lanchesters
162 Fulham Palace Road
London W6 9ER
www.constablerobinson.com

First published in the UK by Constable,
an imprint of Constable & Robinson Ltd., 2011

Excerpt from *Mervyn Peake* by John Watney
(Michael Joseph, 1976) reprinted by permission of Marcus Watney

Excerpt from *The Naked Civil Servant* by Quentin Crisp
(Jonathan Cape, 1968) reprinted by permission of
the Estate of Quentin Crisp

Excerpt from *1945: The Dawn Came Up Like Thunder* by Tom Pocock
(Collins, 1983) reprinted by permission of Penny Pocock

Excerpt from Introduction to *Mervyn Peake: The Man and his Art*
(ed. G. Peter Winnington) (Peter Owen, 2006) by Michael Moorcock
reprinted by permission of Michael Moorcock

Excerpt of 'The Listeners' by Walter de la Mare © 1912, reprinted by
permission of The Trustees of Walter de la Mare and the Society of
Authors as their representatives

A copy of the British Library Cataloguing in
Publication data is available from the British Library

ISBN 978-1-84901-511-0

Printed and bound in the EU

1 3 5 7 9 10 8 6 4 2

MIX
Paper from
responsible sources
FSC® C018575

For Scarlett, Titus and Jack – love always.

The vastest things are those we may not learn.
We are not taught to die, nor to be born,
Nor how to burn with love.
How pitiful is our enforced return
To those small things we are the masters of.

The Vastest Things Are Those We May Not Learn,
Mervyn Peake

It all began on a rainy September morning in 1936.

I've often pictured the high-ceilinged studio at the Westminster School of Art, transparent dots settling on the broad skylight above, like a Seurat. I see the students in their coloured smocks, red-mouthed women with sharp bobs, men in baggy trousers. I hear smoky laughter from the full-figured models and, up above, I see the dark skies of London spoiling for the start of autumn.

I see my father leaning over the clay, shaping it with his dexterous fingers. I see my mother walk nervously into the room. It was her first day at art school. She was seventeen. I know about this moment, how it was love at first sight.

Introduction

I haven't seen my father for forty years and my mother for twenty-five, yet not a day goes by without my thinking of them. They pop in and out of my head with a comforting regularity as I look around me and wonder what they would make of the world. My mother, Maeve Gilmore, was a painter and my father, Mervyn Peake, a novelist, painter, poet and illustrator. If he'd been just one of these things I sometimes think his life might have turned out differently. He has never been easy to place. To some he is the author of the Gormenghast trilogy, to others the illustrator of classics they loved as a child. Some know him as a poet and many don't know him at all. I knew him as a father, and as a father his talents were as great as any line drawing he ever sketched or sentence he ever wrote.

The first few years of my life were wonderfully happy. It seemed I inhabited an enchanted playground, where all the wonders of the world were there, before my eyes; a place where creativity, love and laughter were all you needed for a contented and satisfied soul. Our life abruptly altered when my father became ill. Beginning with a nervous breakdown, it ended with Parkinson's disease, the final diagnosis taking years to discover. It changed him from a cheerful, easy-going man into a frightened stranger, locked into his own private nightmare – a place too far away for me to reach.

In my small world, as the youngest child and only daughter, I was protected from too much pain by a fierce respect for childhood – nothing was allowed to ruin that crucial and fleeting moment. Life for Mervyn and Maeve was much harder than they ever let on and deep down I knew this but, because outwardly they appeared light-hearted and optimistic, I allowed myself to be fooled. Twelve of my father's fifty-seven years were spent in and out of mental institutions and during that time I lived in a haze of confusion, believing that nervous breakdowns and mental hospitals were just a part of life.

Since this book is primarily about my parents I should declare at once that I adored them. I didn't adore them *because* they were my parents, but because they were charming, loving, generous-hearted people, and an absolute joy to be around. With a surfeit of creativity surrounding me wherever I turned, little money and a healthy disregard for convention, an outsider might quite rightly describe our household as bohemian. I saw it only as a munificent and passionate sanctuary, where ideas were everything and love was the key.

The sprawling Victorian house I grew up in is engraved on my mind forever as the scene of more happiness and more despair than anywhere I lived before or have lived since. When my paternal grandparents died, they left their house to my father and, in 1953, when I was four, we moved from Chelsea to the Surrey suburbs. For the next seven years

3

it signified a period in time that was neatly sliced in two, the first half idyllic, the second bewildering and sad.

In 1960 we moved back to Chelsea and life changed again, and for the better. London in the 1960s was a place with a romance all of its own. Optimism clung to the air, a sense of daring made anything seem possible, as if everything were being experienced for the first time. The films, art, theatre, music and fashion were so exciting and inventive you felt yourself to be a participant in a pageant of kaleidoscopic colour. For a time, Mervyn was central to the spirit of this era. While he was languishing in bleak hospitals all over the country, Penguin Books republished the Gormenghast trilogy and, with a fervour, his books were read, dissected and loved by a mass of people in a way he'd never know, never have believed was possible. The books became essential reading, part of the very fabric of a generation's combined memory, and of this I am incredibly proud.

During this difficult time my mother, with a stubborn refusal to give in to self-pity or gloom, created an atmosphere at home that was thrillingly glamorous and alive. Her parties were legendary occasions. Writers, painters, poets and publishers would talk, drink and dance the night away until the early hours, and I can't remember my teenage years without conjuring up an image of our house echoing with the sounds of people having fun.

I have spent my whole life wanting to protect my father. I didn't know that until I began to write this book. Introduced to strangers with my pedigree thrown in as an icebreaker, I long to run away. The complexities of the opening line 'Mervyn Peake's daughter' create a minefield of awkward-ness and embarrassment. Will they stare at me blankly, will they say something clever or will they be nice? I never know. The reason I wanted to protect him, and still do, is because his illness was so awful and pervasive that, as a child, I saw him unable to protect himself. He shrank before my eyes and I felt it my job to straighten him up, to shield him from those who might want to hurt him, to protect this towering man – my hero – from the world.

I don't exaggerate when I say that Maeve and Mervyn's life was one of extremes, the greatest of happiness and the lowest of despair, but with a love so deep and a friendship so enduring it allowed them to believe they'd been lucky. They retained a lack of world-weariness and cynicism that to a child was magical. It was not borne out of naivety but of something else – a belief in people and a genuine love of life.

I have tried to recapture the feeling of a time that is drifting farther and farther away, but for now seems as close as ever. Despite the sadness that coloured our lives, I can only look back with fondness at a time that, unrealistic as it may sound, was glorious. I knew then, as I know now, that what I witnessed was unique.

Chinese Whispers

Behind the compound walls stood six identical grey stone houses, built for the missionaries and their families. Beyond lay China. In one of these double-shuttered, three-storeyed houses, the fourth one along, nearest the tennis court, Mervyn sat drawing at the dining-room table. When I visualise my father as a child, I see him at this table, lost in concentration, an endlessly replenished supply of paper, pencils and crayons spread in front of him, as he draws anything, real and imagined, that he sees. From the moment he could clasp a pencil his parents recognised their son's precocious talent, and encouraged him in his passionate love of drawing. I know that the constant interruptions for meals irritated Mervyn. The obligatory tidying away of pencils and paper to make way for another round of food was to him a hated irrelevance. I'm told he had to be dragged from the table to go to bed. I see him glancing out of the dining-room window, his senses bombarded by the sights and sounds of Tientsin, northern China, where he lived until he was twelve.

It was a happy childhood, a lively, affectionate home with his Congregationalist medical missionary parents, 'Doc' and

Bessie, and elder brother Lonnie, a conventional, middle-class upbringing in the most unconventional of settings, and the very English wordplay, puns and imagery Doc used in his everyday speech were to influence my father for the rest of his life. Mervyn was fascinated by his father's work. Every day on his way to school – by mule and, later, bicycle – he passed hordes of injured people queuing for Doc's surgery, and the cure that would miraculously heal them. Doc performed over a thousand operations a year with Bessie, a nurse, and local assistants by his side, speaking Mandarin to his local assistants, training them in all aspects of medicine. Sometimes Mervyn hid in the viewers' gallery, surreptitiously watching his father performing his operations, once fainting as he watched Doc sawing through the leg of a young Chinaman, the severed limb being carried off on a tray of sawdust.

I would give anything to have known Doc. Whenever his name was mentioned there was a change of texture to the conversation, and the warmth his name provoked made me sorry I never met him. One of ten children, Ernest Cromwell Peake was born in Madagascar in 1874 to missionary parents. A slow-talking, sweet-natured man, he read medicine at Edinburgh University, said goodbye to his parents and, aged twenty-four, embarked on a journey that took him slowly and perilously up the Yangtze river and into China. He didn't see his family again for fifteen years. For one lonely year, he didn't speak to another European. The first Mandarin he learned, 'Have you had your rice today?' being the Chinese equivalent of 'Greetings'.

Four years on, and by now speaking Mandarin fluently, he lived and worked in the Western medicine centre he had set up in Hengchow, in the central Hunan province. On a break from his busy practice, his lingering loneliness finally disappeared when he met Amanda Elizabeth Powell (Bessie), an assistant missionary, and in 1903, five months after their first meeting, they married in Hong Kong. In 1904, their first son, Leslie (Lonnie), was born.

During a summer leave seven years later, in the same mountain resort of Kuling, Central Southern China, where Doc and Bessie had first met – a place so remote and inaccessible that both communist Mao Tse-Tung and nationalist Chiang Kai-shek sought refuge there at various times in their careers – the family awaited the birth of Mervyn. Bessie had a weak heart and it was thought that the mountain air would do her good. She had given birth to still-born twin daughters some time earlier and it was important that she rest. A few days after my father's birth on 9 July 1911, sudden and bloody revolution broke out. As the Peking-based Manchu and the Chinese battled it out in flaming Hankow, Doc set off to join the Red Cross. The number of casualties was enormous and there was huge loss of life. In improvised hospitals and on a commandeered, privately owned steam yacht, Doc and his comrades treated the wounded until the defeated Manchu retreated to Peking and Doc could rejoin his family.

Even so, it was still not safe enough for them to return to their out-station home in Hengchow, and when they finally did go back, Mervyn was already five months old. They were not to stay long. The revolution made life too dangerous for foreigners in Hunan province and, with great sadness at leaving the place where Doc had lived since 1899, the surgery, their many friends and the exotic-fruited, flowered and herbed garden he and Bessie had planted, they, their two sons and their belongings sailed a thousand

8

miles north. Doc was to take over as director of the MacKenzie Memorial Hospital, Tientsin. It was there that Mervyn was to spend his formative years.

When Maeve and Mervyn
Were Young

To learn all he could of England, his homeland, Mervyn read *News from Afar*, *Chums* and *Boys' Own Paper*. He studied the work of his hero, illustrator Stanley L. Wood, who was such an influence that, in Mervyn's first published piece, 'Ways of Travelling', for the London Missionary Society's magazine, an 'L' is proudly inserted in the byline – 'written and illustrated by Mervyn L. Peake of North China aged 10-and-a-half'. He read adventure books, and devoured *Treasure Island* until he knew almost every line of it by heart, never imagining that thirty years later he would be commissioned to illustrate the book he had loved so much as a boy.

In the two pages he wrote of a proposed memoir, he describes the incongruity of Tientsin Grammar School.

It had nothing to do with China. It might have been flown over in a piece from Croydon. It faced the dusty street. Its windows were mouths that shouted, 'I know I'm ugly, and I like it'. There it stood, horrid and ugly among the sweet-stalls on the wide road. The rickshaws would rattle by in the sun, while we tried to remember the name of the longest river in England, the date of Charles II's accession, or where one put the decimal point. I remember only the lady teachers. I think they were all lady teachers, except the headmaster, and a sprightly devil-may-care sort of man who took Latin, and whom we could see the headmaster and his staff thought too flippant. I saw him fourteen or fifteen years later in a train in Surbiton. The life had gone out of him. I remembered in a flash as I saw him how he had kept me in one night because of my backwardness, and how, instead of punishing me, I spent the long summer evening happily bowling to him in the big American recreation ground. What a huge desert that ground was. On Sunday afternoon on the way back from Sunday School I would watch the huge Americans playing baseball without a smile on their faces. Great men, fifteen feet high at least with clubs to crack the devil's head for ever, dressed up like armadillos. How they would run. From base to base they sped, crouching as they ran, with their bodies slanting over like yachts to an angle of 45 degrees.

The ancient traditions and rigidity of the customs, the visits to Peking to see the Forbidden City and the Great Wall Spirit, were all to influence Mervyn's writing and drawing for the rest of his life. Without China, Gormenghast couldn't have existed. It was an exotic, pulsating, juxtaposed world of conformist religion and superstition, rickshaws and dragons, tiffin and cricket, with an underlying emphasis on kindness and good manners. He was taught a way of living, and a

11

way of treating people, that remained intact when everything around him had crumbled, and survived until the day he died. I know that the sights, smells and rituals of the arcane world he grew up in were always in his blood, and I know that the memories were almost too big to share.

In 1923 Doc, Bessie and Mervyn left China and travelled to England for a furlough, but they never returned. Bessie's health was deteriorating and Doc decided once he was back in England to resign from the London Missionary Society and take up practice in Surrey. Mervyn joined Lonnie, who had been sent back to England to be educated some years previously. They went to Eltham College, Kent, a school for the sons of missionaries, where Doc and six of his brothers had gone before them. Lonnie and Mervyn were both sporty and popular, and their time at boarding school was perfectly agreeable. Mervyn's basic, lavatorial humour and ability to caricature his teachers went down well with the other boys, but he was often caned for minor offences. A former pupil described him at this time as 'always dreamily in trouble'. While Lonnie did well at school, Mervyn was a terrible student, so poor that he was nearly expelled for his lack of progress. A teacher's meeting was held and it was only the art master's intervention that saved him. Recognising Mervyn's exceptional talent, he argued that expelling a future famous old boy would do nothing to enhance the school's reputation.

After leaving Eltham College with nothing to show for it except his First XI colours and a life-long friend, Mervyn enrolled at Croydon Art School, but left after a few weeks, having been accepted on a five-year course at the Royal Academy Schools in Piccadilly. He completed three and a half. In the summer of 1933, when he was twenty-two, his dream of adventure came to fruition when he was invited by Eric Drake, an inspirational English teacher who had taught him at Eltham, to help build an artists' colony on the island of Sark. It turned out to be a place perfectly suited to his quixotic temperament. He could paint all day, which he did on occasions in the nude, on the beach, with just a sombrero to keep the sun off his face or the rain off his head. There was a voluptuous local girl known for her generosity, gnarled Sarkese men and wind-bent trees to paint, a tin shack to sleep in and a pet cormorant to love. Reckless by nature, Mervyn would cycle along La Coupée, a narrow, winding, unmade road, pedalling furiously downhill, arms outstretched, while, on either side of him, a precipitous drop fell away for three hundred feet, with no railing to save him from the often angry sea below. There was also the gallery he had helped build in which to exhibit. It was a wonderful existence, and might have gone on being so had the principal of the Westminster School of Art not visited Sark, seen Mervyn's pictures at a mixed exhibition and immediately offered him a teaching post. The reviews had been glowing: 'An outstanding exhibitor is Mervyn Peake, who won the Hacker Porticut Prize at the Royal Academy Schools in 1931, and has exhibited at the Royal Academy, the Redfern Gallery and the London Group. His chalk and charcoal studies are masterful.' Another reviewer, equally enthusiastic, wrote: 'In some cases the work was stamped with something approaching genius. This was particularly so in the case of Mervyn Peake, a young man still on the sunny side of twenty-two, whose versatility and imagination place him in a class of his own.'

*

I know far less about my mother's childhood. What I do know was all learned in one never-to-be-forgotten conversation when I was seventeen or so. I had gone into her bedroom one early winter's evening at that melancholy hour between five and six, a little before she poured her first gin and tonic. She was lying on top of her tall brass bed and, as I lay down beside her, she began to talk spontaneously of her childhood. Born in 1918 to a staunch Roman Catholic family, she had grown up in Acre Lane, Brixton, an area at the time popular with prosperous professionals. Each house had, as the name implies, an acre of land attached to it. In the huge double-fronted villa lived her parents, three brothers and two sisters, an ancient retainer nursery maid and a variety of other servants. An elderly African Grey flew around the house, resting on curtains, landing on people's heads or sitting in his cage impersonating members of the household. He mimicked my Grandmother Matty so impeccably that the same game was played over and over again. 'Robert! Robert! We're ready to leave now,' he would call to the chauffeur. 'Robert, where are you?' Robert, rushing to his mistress's call, fell for it every time.

Uniformed staff stood to attention at breakfast time, food at the ready under silver salvers, but Miss Maeve could never be tempted by more than a slice of toast. The ham and eggs, kidneys and bacon, porridge and kippers were too much so early in the morning. There appeared to be staff for every room: butler, cook, scullery maid, chambermaid, parlour maid, under parlour maid, seamstress and valet. They ran the house with precision. Maeve spoke of her fondness for them, of sitting by the open fire in the kitchen chatting to Cookie as she prepared yet another meal for the

14

family. She spoke of 'taking the waters' on their annual holidays in the spa towns of eastern Europe, and of travelling in the dickey of the family Buick with their new chauffeur, Penfold, leading the fleet of cars that carried the luggage and the rest of the family. She spoke of riding side-saddle along Rotten Row in the mornings, and language-learning in the afternoons; of being escorted to balls by earnest suitors, a chaperone close by to keep an eye on her; of family boxes at the theatre.

Taken to see Ivor Novello perform in a musical comedy, by his mother, Mrs Novello Davies, a family friend, Maeve left the theatre in love for the first time. Returning to boarding school and refusing to eat, she was carted off to a specialist by a concerned nun, but never revealed the cause of her emaciated frame to the doctor, who recommended, with great sensitivity, she have her tonsils removed.

I had never met my maternal grandparents, so was quite unprepared for what I heard. I saw my parents only as themselves, attached to no one but us. My mother spoke of her past life in a calm, flat tone, as though incredulous that once upon a time she had lived like this. The days she described so vividly were so far removed from the life we led as to be almost unimaginable. I lay there in silence, willing her on, wanting nothing to interrupt her outpouring. It was as though she were remembering for herself, as if she needed to believe that this short period had really happened, and to exorcise a pain she had harboured all these years.

She was the youngest and prettiest of six children, and her doctor father worshipped his youngest child, who had inherited his brains and good looks. But Maeve was desperately hurt by the disparity in the way he treated her and her mother, Matty. Born with neither good looks nor

15

great intelligence, Matty had a sweetness crushed and belittled at every turn. Her attraction lay in the enormous wealth she inherited from her newspaper-magnate grand-father, Henry Lascelles-Carr, owner of the *Western Mail* and the *News of the World*. Maeve spoke of her mother's tinkling laugh, her slender wrists and ankles, her affectionate and playful disposition. She spoke of her immense love for her mother, and mixed feelings of admiration and antipathy for her clever, enigmatic and sentimental Irish father. She described herself sitting stiffly on his lap as he played 'Danny Boy' and 'The Wearing of the Green' on the piano with tears streaming down his face, and she spoke of her ambivalence to his tears. She wanted her father to recognise the small daily hurts he inflicted on his wife, who brushed them off with the pretence that she hadn't even noticed. She spoke of the comfort of her nightly prayers; how, as a small child, she would kneel by her bed, praying that she might contract a fatal illness, so her parents would be forced to sit by her side and, as she lay dying, would be reunited by a common love for their child. She imagined their eyes meeting as her father suddenly understood that it was his wife he had loved all along. As I listened, it was clear she felt disloyal and angry with herself for having admired her father, but that, despite herself, she did.

A Winter Wedding

O ur photograph albums sat in a decrepit pyramid that I occasionally looked at as a child, but scrutinised with more intensity as the years went by. The black and white photographs are largely unposed, and all have a strangely ethereal quality to them. They begin with pictures of Mervyn as a young boy in China and end in the Priory Hospital fifty-six years later. One picture shows him as a ten-year-old cub scout. It always seemed so odd somehow, so hard to imagine him dib-dibbing and bob-a-jobbing in such a remote landscape. Back straight, hands in pockets, his left foot is placed way in front of his right, as though making sure that at least one of his feet was planted firmly on the ground. He has a sensitive, intelligent face and is so handsome that, as a seven-year-old girl, I would look at this photograph, hoping one day to have a cub-scout boyfriend as handsome as he was.

There is only one picture of my mother as a child, and I would gaze at it sometimes for its peculiarly old-fashioned quality. A tiny girl with a Louise Brooks bob wears a very short, white lace dress, the legs that hold her body upright as skinny as two matchsticks. She is dwarfed by a gigantic doll's pram. Her miniature face in profile, she clasps the handle of the pram as a stout nanny in full, ankle-length uniform watches over her. As the story of her childhood unfolded that evening, so the picture confirmed the differences between my parents' early lives. The ease of the poses captured in China could have been taken today; the lone picture of Maeve seemed from another century. Time moves on as the pages turn, but the mood remains the same, a light-hearted, illusory mood that seems almost timeless. Images of Mervyn clasping a branch above his head like the enormous antlers of a deer, now full face, now profile, the same branch, but held differently. In some his eyes are closed, in others, open, but in every frame he looks at one with the antlers, as though they are growing from him. Other photographs from the same day have him lying languorously in the branches of a tall oak tree, as if that's where he belongs.

The wedding photographs are the only formal images that the albums contain. Two stiff, uncomfortable young people stare nervously at the camera, as though aching to peel off their clothes and run away – from everyone: guests, family, attention. Neither had wanted any fuss, but had been worn down by family pressure to marry where generations of Gilmores had married – St James's, Spanish Place, in the heart of London's West End. Mervyn dressed for the first and last time in a morning suit, black leather shoes gleaming in the winter air, gloves and top hat clasped tightly to his chest. Maeve is in oyster-coloured velvet. The dress still hangs in my wardrobe, the velvet as soft as on the day she married, the seventeen-inch waist measured and corroborated to quell my disbelief.

Physically, Mervyn and Maeve were very different, and if you didn't know them well, their temperaments could seem very different, too. Mervyn was a flamboyant, confident man, at home in any surroundings in which he found himself, and with the combination of his Welsh mother's dark, brooding looks and English father's height, he cut a striking figure. His hair, worn much longer than was usual for the time, his unconventional and colourful clothes, together with the gold, hooped earrings he wore in both ears, made him one of the well-known figures in Soho and Fitzrovia in the thirties. His looks may have been brooding but his temperament was anything but. He was flirtatious and good fun, with an earthy sense of humour and a twinkle in his eye.

In stature and colouring my mother was his exact opposite. She was pale, fair and extremely slight and, unlike Mervyn, she was nervy, and desperately shy. She also dressed in a highly individual way for the times, with red espadrilles that tied all the way up her legs, skin tight Chinese dresses with high collars and gashes on either side, and fitted tweed hunting jackets worn over floor-length cotton skirts. Gigantic drop earrings hung from her ears and huge Spanish combs held up her hair but, apart from the unconventionality of her dress, she had none of the natural ease of my father. Yet her sense of humour was as quick and just as abstract as his. In Mervyn, she saw the poet she had always dreamed of; in Maeve, he saw everything a poet could ever want. Diana Gardner, a former student of Mervyn's at the Westminster School of Art, recalled them at this time. 'He gave off a sense of sentient vitality, as if he lived a "little extra", and his senses were also a "little extra". Here was the perfect Byronic romantic figure – jet black hair bursting upwards from a high forehead and a long narrow face in which were embedded bright blue eyes and sharply cut incisions in either side of a full, yet narrow and sensitive mouth. It is probably now quite obvious that the female students found him irresistible for, apart from his fascinating looks, he always seemed, while sitting beside any one of them, teaching, to be wholly interested in that one alone. It was apparent that he liked women, although he was also popular with the male teachers and students.

'Mervyn mentioned almost in passing that he was going to be married in two months' time – and this was proffered by someone who had been accepted as a kind of perpetual Don Juan!' Diana remembered. 'It was an equal surprise to hear that the woman chosen was also a student at the Westminster – but not known to anyone in the life class because she worked quietly downstairs in Eric Shilsky's sculpture class.'

During a break, Diana and other students went to the sculpture room to be introduced to Maeve by a diffident Mervyn. Maeve had 'her gold hair scraped back into a knot and pinned, and with two-inch gold rings hanging from small ear lobes, she could be recognised as an artist's archetypal human being: someone from a Florentine painting'.

It went without saying that Maeve Gilmore would marry well, and she did marry well, but in a wildly different way from what her parents expected or hoped for. Although irresistible to Maeve, Mervyn was anything but irresistible to her parents. Frightened by the intensity of their daughter's passion for a man who was never going to make any money, she was sent to Germany to learn the language and, if all went to plan, forget this impoverished artist. A life of 'making do' wasn't what they had in mind for their youngest and most beautiful child and, after a while, with a few hundred miles between them, she would, they were sure, forget.

For six months she lived in a castle owned by a cheerful widow, Baroness Von Norbeck, travelling back and forth to Bonn every day for her art classes. While there, she witnessed Hitler speaking at a parade, and never forgot the terrifying magnetism he held over the crowd. Maeve and Mervyn wrote every day of those painful months spent apart (the letters were destroyed during the war when a bomb hit her parents' new house in Chelsea Square) and when Maeve returned home, she refused to consider marrying anyone else – ever. She would become a nun, live in a closed-order convent and bid farewell to everything and everyone if the answer was no. Her adoring parents eventually gave in. Mervyn's lack of money and address (a warehouse in Hester Road, Battersea) and his bohemian ways couldn't disguise his lovely nature and passionately focused approach to work, and it wasn't long before they became very fond of their prospective son-in-law.

For all the differences in their upbringings – Maeve's spoilt and sophisticated, Mervyn's modest and unique – my parents were alike. They were made of the same stuff, and on 1 December 1937, Miss Maeve Patricia Mary Theresa Gilmore married Mr Mervyn Laurence Peake.

They moved to Primrose Mansions, to a flat overlooking Battersea Park, where my nineteen-year-old mother described herself at this time as knowing nothing of anything – cooking, cleaning, conversation, life. There was no one alive more boring than her, she said. Mervyn, by now making quite a name for himself, was proudly introducing his new bride to a very different world. At first, intimidated by the people she met, people she knew by reputation, she was painfully shy. But the first and, at the time, most famous poet she was introduced to, Walter de la Mare, immediately put her at her ease with his gentle, friendly manner. He had invited Mervyn to tea at his house in the country so he and his wife could meet Maeve. And slowly, through her husband's belief in her, she began to acquire a quiet self-confidence that was to remain with her for the rest of her life.

In 1938 they moved from Battersea to Maida Vale, where they painted side by side on two floors of a rented house, living on the money they earned by selling their pictures and with some help from Maeve's parents. Patricia Herington, a neighbour in Randolph Avenue, remembered those days:

Our back gates opened on to a large communal garden. One afternoon my mother washed my hair, gave me a clean frock and sent me out there. I didn't yet know the neighbouring children. One or two spoke to me and told me there was to be a party. I suppose my mother knew and hoped I might get scooped up and included. That didn't happen. All the children disappeared and I stayed on my bench feeling left out and too ashamed to go home. Your parents saw me from the window and came down to rescue me. Once upstairs, they gave me strawberries and ice cream. The afternoon changed colour. These two wonderful beings liked me. And Mervyn – my exciting artist friend – had chosen to paint me and not one of the other children. A tiny incident but of enormous importance to that little girl who was me. You see how kind your parents were.

Their flat was a delight – especially to a child. There

was something lovely to look at wherever you turned. Your father painted vines, flowers and birds all over the doors and on one a life-sized portrait of your beautiful mother with her long blonde hair, dressed, I now realise as a nymph. Because I was keen to become an artist, Mervyn made me up a little sketchbook. At the time I was in my Dutch phase and obsessed with producing pictures of little girls in fly-away bonnets, boys in baggy trousers and bowls of stiff tulips. With patience and understanding he got me to look at the world around me as well as the one within. As we studied a geranium together, he persuaded me to try and copy the stems and explained that it was the life moving through the plant which twisted its shape in different ways. He said although it was still, in its pot, you could imagine it dancing. In September of that year, war was declared and very soon afterwards we were all dispersed. Two special people who made me feel cherished and safe went out of my life, though not out of my memory.

With the war approaching, Mervyn and Maeve decided to pack up and move again, this time to the country. They rented a small, damp house in Warningcamp, Sussex, a mile from Burpham, where Doc and Bessie had retired, and awaited my father's call-up papers and the birth of their first child, my brother Sebastian.

Among the letters I inherited from my mother when she died were several from Mervyn to his mother-in-law. Most mentioned socks.

November 1939

Dear Mrs Gilmore,

How can I tell you how much I admire and appreciate my pink socks? 'Pink' is a feeble word for the colours that distil about my ankles, which are getting more and more spoiled. They are really lovely (my socks, not my ankles) and with the tie Ruth [Maeve's sister] has made for me, I feel quite 'set up' aesthetically. Not only from the decorative standpoint, but functionally, they are perfect. In actual fact, they fit me better than any I have ever had, the heel sliding beautifully on and gripping on my own heel resiliently and firmly.

I admire your craftsmanship. The cigarettes have been, as I'm sure you know from past experience of my nicotine habit, very much appreciated, too. I am smoking one at this moment.

It will be very nice if you can manage to get along this way when the baby is born. Maeve is feeling pretty rotten these days and is longing for the suspense to be over. It has been most kind of you to help her so much with your very necessary and beautiful gifts for the baby, many of which have taken you and Ruth many hours of work. Your generosity in regard to the nursing home has been an invaluable help and kindness. My own resources are practically nil, as the Westminster, though open, is working with a skeleton staff. I hope it will put on a few muscles one day. Selling a few pictures here and there doesn't really make much difference, and I only appreciate the teaching work I had now that I've lost it. It is possible that I will be appointed as a war artist as Kenneth Clarke, who is director of the N. Gallery, is chairman of the committee which the

24

Ministry of Information has set up, and who will choose the artists. But one never knows how long one has to wait. I am also being kept waiting by publishers from whom I may get commissions to illustrate some classics.

However, I suppose things will recover. I did not mean this letter to contain any allusions to the seamy-er side of life, but rather to impress upon you my very sincerest wishes for Christmas and 1940.

With love from Mervyn.

Sapper Peake, Gunner 1597577, was called up on 29 July 1940. 'Get your hair cut, you look like a bloody poet,' said the sergeant at his first parade. Mervyn was a willing but hopelessly inept soldier, bored rigid by the pettiness of army life, but he got on well with his comrades, whom he drew at every opportunity. Despite a letter from Augustus John to the War Office, recommending 'Mr Mervyn Peake as a draughtsman of great distinction, who might be most suitably employed in war records', and despite John's letter to Mervyn, remarking that 'so far one has seen little but the comic side of warfare treated by alleged draughtsmen. You, like Goya, are interested in the serious', his longing to be of what he considered 'real use' during the war never happened. Instead, he was a driving instructor (with no driving licence and no knowledge of engines) and a cookhouse orderly. It was a dreadful waste of talent and an enormous disappointment to Mervyn. 'If they put the wrong people in the wrong jobs at the bum-end of the army, they probably do at the scalp end,' he wrote to his friend Gordon Smith.

It was at this time that he began writing *Titus Groan*, the first book in the Gormenghast trilogy. Any free moment would be spent in the barracks writing in small red exercise pads and publishers' dummies, which were then sent home to Maeve for safe-keeping. She would type them up and keep them by her at all times, saying that if a bomb should be making its way to Sussex, there were three essentials she would grab when making a dash for it – babies, nappies, manuscript. There were two babies now. Sebastian and Fabian. Fabian, delivered by Wendy in the Peter Pan nursing home in Rustington, had been born in April 1942 and, as Mervyn was moved around the country fulfilling his army duties, Maeve stayed in Sussex, looking after their two small sons.

In May 1942 a telegram arrived informing Maeve that her husband had had a nervous breakdown. He was sent to the Military Hospital Neurosis Centre in Southport and, in 1943, was discharged from the army as surplus to requirements. During this time, he made a recorder from bamboo on which he learned to play 'Plaisir d'amour' and 'Jesu, Joy of Man's Desiring', pieces my mother often played on the piano after my father died.

He had so longed to contribute in a real way, and a few weeks after the war ended it seemed at last to be possible. Mervyn was commissioned by the *Leader* magazine to accompany Tom Pocock, a young journalist, to Germany where Tom would write as Mervyn drew, each depicting the aftermath of the war. Mervyn wrote to Maeve: 'You know I will do all that is in me to do what was in our minds when we decided, through your insight, that it was for me to make records of what humanity suffered through war. I will not forget the reasons which prompted me to try and go to where people suffer. I will miss you desperately, but I will be proud to do something which we both believe in.'

In his memoir, *1945: The Dawn Came Up Like Thunder*, Tom Pocock describes their first meeting and subsequent trip:

The Peakes were then living in a residential studio in Glebe Place off the King's Road in Chelsea, but our first meetings were in another, which he rented for a few shillings a week in Trafalgar Studios, a gaunt block in Manresa Road. This was Bohemia as I had always imagined it: the enormous, high-ceilinged studio with its great, grimy window, stacked with canvases and reeking of oil paint and turpentine. Jars stuffed with brushes, a palette bright with abstract dabs and swirls of paint, and an open bottle of cheap sherry, were prominent details of décor. There was also, as expected, a beautiful girl in attendance. This was Maeve Gilmore, Mervyn's wife, whose corn-coloured hair, wide-set eyes and air of content, made her seem to me the goddess Ceres incarnate.

Mervyn Peake, then aged thirty-three, was a lean, slightly stooped man with black, sprouting hair and a narrow, deep-lined face in which dark, troubled eyes were set close. His manner was friendly, slightly diffident; gentle, but also masculine. One could sense that he had been an appallingly helpless soldier – he was reputed to have saluted with his left hand when he remembered to salute at all – and as our preparations progressed it became obvious that the little disciplines and formalities of military life, which I took for granted, were to him bewildering irrelevancies ... but Mervyn was as professional and efficient in the assembling of his

27

artist's materials as he had been bemused by the logistics of our expedition. His dark sombre good looks and the deep-set troubled eyes might have belonged to a most forceful person but he was intensely gentle . . . a delightful and generous companion.

The photograph album shows pictures of Mervyn in 1945, dressed in an army greatcoat, sitting on a pile of broken bricks in occupied Germany, or standing against a wall with crumbling, cratered buildings in the background, the ubiquitous cigarette in his mouth, pencil in hand, recording the awful destruction in a sketchbook.

He wrote to Maeve from near Wiesbaden:

Most dearly beloved-oh-my darling girl –
What a terrific lot has happened since I wrote to you from Paris – yet I was in Paris this morning. I am now on the river near Wiesbaden, and tomorrow we are jeeping to Bonn.

After the impression I have received here, of the way the Germans feel towards the Americans, and presumably towards the English too (we're in an American zone at the moment) I don't feel too keen on introducing myself to one.

It is true that today a few peasants waved from the fields, and one or two oldish people bowed good morning and a few girls smiled hopefully, but in the main it would be impossible to believe were one not to see them. They are no more. They are relics. Terrible as the bombing of London was, it is absolutely nothing – nothing compared with this unutterable desolation. Imagine Chelsea in fragments with not one single house with any more than a few weird-shaped walls where it once stood, and you will get an idea in miniature of what Mannheim and Wiesbaden are like – yet these are the only two that we have seen, save for the broken streets of every small town we passed through on our jeep ride here today. The Ruhr, to which we are going tomorrow, is reputed to be the worst – but how could it be worse than what I've seen today.

In June 1945, two months after the British Army liberated Belsen, Mervyn went to the concentration camp. The wooden huts the inmates had lived and died in had been razed to the ground, and those inmates still – barely – alive moved to the former SS tank barracks. He drew them, as one by one they died. That day was nothing in comparison to the suffering these people had experienced, but to be present at the death of a stranger, to witness the barbarity of what the Nazis left behind was to confront evil. I'm told that after a while he appeared to be as he had always been, but the experience had done something to him and was to haunt him forever. It was the catalyst for what was to come.

Tom Pocock described how he had left Mervyn at the main gates of the camp one morning and promised to collect him there in the afternoon . . .

When I returned to the gates of Belsen, Mervyn was waiting and climbed into the Humber staff car beside me. He had a sketch-pad in his hand and, as he turned its pages, I could see drawing after drawing of skeletal figures. On the last page, he had neatly written some verse and he asked me to read it.

The poem was expanded and later published in a collection of Mervyn's poetry, *The Glassblowers*:

THE CONSUMPTIVE, BELSEN 1945

If seeing her an hour before her last
Weak cough into all blackness I could yet
Be held by chalk-white walls, and by the great
Ash coloured bed,
And the pillows hardly creased
By the tapping of her little cough-jerked head –
If such can be a painter's ecstasy,
(Her limbs like pipes, her head a china skull)
Then where is mercy?
And what
Is this my traffic? For my schooled eyes see
The ghost of a great painting, line and hue,
In this doomed girl of tallow?
O Jesus! Has the world so white a yellow
As lifts her head by but a breath from linen
In the congested yet empty world.
Of plaster, cotton and a little marl?
Than pallor what is there more terrible?
There lay the gall
Of that dead mouth of the world.
And at death's centre a torn garden trembled
In which her eyes like great hearts of black water
Shone in their wells of bone,
Brimmed to the well-heads of the coughing girl,
Pleading through history in that white garden;
And very wild, upon the head's cheekbones,

30

As on high ridges in an icy dew,
Burned the sharp roses.

Her agony slides through me: I am glass
That grief can find no grip
Save for a moment when the quivering lip
And the coughing weaker than the broken wing
That, fluttering, shakes the life from a small bird
Caught me as in a nightmare? Nightmares pass
The image blurs and the quick razor-edge
Of anger dulls, and pity dulls. O God,
That grief so glibly slides! The little badge
On either cheek was gathered from her blood:
Those coughs were her last words. They had no weight
Save that through them was made articulate
Earth's desolation on the alien bed.
Though I be glass, it shall not be betrayed,
That last weak cough of her small, trembling head.

The girl was to haunt Mervyn for years to come.

The dream-like photographs continue. Page after page of Maeve and Mervyn with Sebastian and Fabian, the four of them, the perfect unit, two young boys with two young parents, until I arrive seven years later to alter the dynamics – me, a fat, woollen-bonneted, nine-month-old baby, propped on the hide of Judy, our donkey, with no sign of anyone around to catch me if I topple; pictures of my smiling father, holding me on his shoulder, in his arms, above his head, by his side.

Then come the pages of sadness, the pages I prefer to skip over. Photographs of my mother looking at my father as though he were a small child she must constantly fret over, cling to, prop up. Mervyn looks ninety, Maeve fifty. They are in the grounds of the Priory Hospital, a few months before he is taken away to a place where he is cared for properly. Maeve is holding Mervyn's hand. He looks at the camera. She stares at him, her eyes are defeated, she attempts a smile. The collars of their coats are turned up.

A Sark Beginning

I was conceived on a brand new brown and tan checked picnic blanket, in the secluded back garden of our house on Sark, the tiny rugged Channel island that makes up the fourth quarter of Jersey, Guernsey, Alderney and Sark. After the war it seemed the perfect place to bring up a young family, so my parents and brothers uprooted and settled in the place where Mervyn had lived so happily as a young man. Before my mother and brothers joined him, and three years before I was so much as a twinkle in their eyes, Mervyn went ahead to make the arrangements for the move.

July 1946

My own sweet wife,

I have been picturing you in my mind, and each time I can get your darling face in focus, and see you clearly, I get a shock of pleasure and pride that you belong to me, and I wonder how I could have left you. I have been loving you deeply and remembering so many lovely things about you. Little Maeve, my dearest one – I am longing for you already. I feel a bit lonely wandering around the place by myself and ache to have you with me.

There is a magnificent attic – very extensive and light – which would make a fine place for the children on rainy days as an alternative to the nursery.

But the flowers! They are a glorious and gorgeous sight. There are infinitely more varieties than I imagined, and many flowering trees. Things are coming up, which were quite invisible before. Huge crimson poppies – six inches across – hydrangeas, lilac, roses galore, and masses of carnations and the grape vine is getting very strong again. I have bought a very big kitchen dresser for £2 and a strong folding table for 4/- at a sale. Everything is so much more fun with you, but I can't have everything I suppose. I do hope fervently that my being away hasn't given you too fatiguing a time with the children. But have you had a chance to do any painting? If you do any, I will be thrilled to see it – oh darling, I do love you so much. I'm sure everything is going to go wonderfully for us. We mustn't rush anything, take things at our own speed and everything will fall into place. People seem so friendly and glad that we are coming. Mrs Bateman is longing to see you again and the children – but nobody can touch me for sheer fervour and excitement to have you as their wife – for it's only me that you married.

They were renting Le Chalet, a large and run-down, but handsome, house where they lived a blissful existence before I made an appearance. One afternoon my mother spotted a newborn baby being pushed along The Avenue, and experienced an overwhelming pang of broodiness.

34

Retracing her steps, she found my father and asked if she could have one, too. He was happy to oblige and, while Sebastian and Fabian were at school, I was conceived, and on a beautiful May day, nine and a half months later, at eight in the morning, I was born, weighing in at a dainty nine pounds.

A new arrival on such a tiny island was quite an event, and my birth was heralded with all the pomp and circumstance usually afforded to a most important baby. The moment my newborn wailing reached the ears of Armand, my family's Moroccan gardener, he threw down his hoe and jumped on his bicycle. Cycling round the three-and-a-half miles of this rugged and mysterious island, he peeled a bell and called out to the 350 inhabitants: 'C'est une fille! C'est une fille!' After two adored but extremely naughty sons, 'C'est une fille!' was just what the doctor ordered.

The pregnancy had been a pretty straightforward affair, with the exception of my mother's revulsion for a harmless yellow cup, and a nocturnal craving for chunks of floury bread spread with thick layers of Dijon mustard. With no hospital and no nurse on the island, a midwife from England had been hired to stay in the house until I was ready to emerge. However, the moment Mervyn and Sister Kilfoyle set eyes on each other at the harbour wall, it was clear this was not going to be a friendship made in heaven. Although an exceptionally kind man, a bossy, unattractive woman was where he drew the line, and the steep drive up the harbour hill in Charlie Perree's horse and carriage was tinged with foreboding.

Waiting for the big day to arrive, Sister Kilfoyle's evenings were whiled away on the veranda. Settling herself down at the cast-iron table, she placed her scrapbook in front of her

35

and carefully opened the bound album to show my parents photograph after photograph of royal weddings and stately homes. She showed them lush gardens, aristocratic prams and silver spoons, and she showed them how and where she'd assisted generations of landed gentry into the world, illustrating perfectly what a comedown a house with no electricity and hand-pumped water was to a woman of her socially superior know-how. Sister Kilfoyle (long since referred to by my father as Sister Tinfoil or Sister Killjoy) was on her way out. A mutual animosity had grown to insurmountable proportions between the two of them, and my mother decided that, immediately after my birth, it would be better if the Sister took her midwifery skills elsewhere.

Days passed and when no baby appeared to have any intention of ever arriving, Sister Kilfoyle demanded swift measures be swung into operation. As she stood scowling at the bottom of the staircase, Maeve was ordered up and down, up and down, faster and faster, until she finally collapsed on the bottom step with exhaustion, and not the slightest hint of a contraction to show for it. She squatted in scalding baths, sipping from glasses of neat gin, and sucked on small lumps of bread soaked in cod liver oil. Saunters round Sark that involved climbing low walls and yanking Sister Kilfoyle's enormous frame over with her also made no impact. As a last resort, Charlie Perree lugged my mother, brothers and Sister Kilfoyle on to his horse and carriage and rode them from Big Sark to Little Sark over the roughest tracks he knew. 'Has the baby come yet?' Fabian enquired after every lurch. Nothing worked – and time was running out. Sister Kilfoyle was booked for two weeks, and ten days were up already, but late into the night of 24 May things started to happen all on their own.

As Maeve continued her lengthy labour in their bedroom, Mervyn was banished to the rest of the house until further notice. While waiting to be summoned by Killjoy, he spent those long hours painting my mother and me a picture of three friendly monsters sitting at a refectory table. The Birthday Breakfast was meant as a joint welcoming and congratulatory present, but his only job, Kilfoyle informed him, was to warm a blanket on the Aga. In his nervy expulsion he forgot all about it, until he smelt singeing and scrutinised the almost perfectly circular hole in the now not so immaculate picnic blanket. Ashamed and apologetic, but at last allowed in, he hurriedly carried what was left of the blanket in one hand and the wet canvas in the other to present his new baby and exhausted wife with his gift. Before he'd even had time to kiss his wife or new daughter, Sister Kilfoyle began screaming at him, almost managing to ruin this joyful moment with her crimson-faced fury. 'Where's your mask, man?' she screeched as her small eyes landed on the canvas. 'Get that germ-laden thing out of here at once!' A whispered and furious row followed. Sister Kilfoyle stormed out, the picture was hung and, germs or no germs, I survived the day.

I don't seem to have sensed the rampant tension all around me since I arrived in the world a contented and jolly baby. It was a wonderful time for everyone. The war was over, Sebastian and Fabian, aged seven and nine, had all the stimulation that a recently occupied island had to offer, including a bunker in the garden built for the occupying German Commandant and his staff. Mervyn had commissions, Maeve had a new baby and I slotted into this world with all the ease of the youngest child. Sebastian and Fabian (or 'the blue-eyed thugs' as Louis MacNeice called them) were wild and remorselessly energetic, fought continuously, perfected their pea-shooting skills and behaved like most boys did in the 1940s. Every evening, after supper and before bedtime, they would escape for one last adventure with their friends Reggie and Phillip, and Maeve would treat herself to a much-needed hour of peace. She called it 'love hour'. It was when she put her feet up, opened the top buttons of her dress and surrounded herself with life's vital accoutrements: a gin and tonic, a baby, a cigarette and a chapter or two of the book she was reading.

I know all this because, thirty-three years later when Maeve was in the Charing Cross Hospital and hanging on to life by a thread, she wrote a story for me, found someone to type it and, a month or two later, I sat on a packing case in my basement and read 'For my darling daughter', written on my birthday, three months before she died.

It was obvious from the start that I was physically different from my parents and brothers. They were all thin, wiry sort of people, with cheekbones, ribs and high foreheads. I must have been a throwback to some hearty peasant girl from another century, as old black and white photographs show me resembling the offspring of a potato farmer, the sort of baby held under the sturdy arm of a farmer's wife that Van Gogh might have painted. From the word go I was a dimpled, rotund creature, with the fine features of both parents hidden under layers of double chins and double knees, enormously happy with my family, and, although I'm sure it doesn't make me a fully rounded person in the eyes of a psychiatrist, that never changed. As I gurgled contentedly in my pram in the garden, my father wrote *Gormenghast* and my mother painted and cooked and lived the days that would turn out to be the happiest of their lives.

A house without animals was a stark and soulless place in the eyes of my parents, and although Chakka, the Black Napoleon (a black cat) and Moby Dick (a white cat) had ended their days as native Londoners, they had uprooted Chloe (a tabby cat), a city girl just entering middle age. After some sulky resistance she had finally learned what it was to be a real cat and, instead of stretching, yawning and curling up on a sofa in Chelsea with all the feral instincts of a snail, now spent her days slightly self-consciously, but nevertheless industriously, clambering up the palm tree that my father had proudly planted. Judy, our ancient, sweet-tempered donkey, when ravaged by the strong Channel winds whipping and lashing at her sturdy, stolid body outside, idled her days inside the house, staring with great sagacity at the bookshelves as though pondering on which to read next. Proust, his twelve volumes spanning the centre of one shelf at perfect eye level, proved the most popular.

The journey to Sark can be terrible. The Channel crossing is notoriously rough and friends from London usually made it just once. But once was all it took for me to be baptised in the sitting room by a priest sent from Guernsey on special dispensation from the Cardinal of Westminster (a concession usually given only to royalty or high-ranking Catholics) to prevent a later life of limbo for the small pagan who had found herself being born on a tiny island with no Catholic church in sight. He sailed on the *Ile de Sercq*, an ancient freighter, which took about an hour to cover the nine or ten miles of treacherous water and dock at the Maseline Harbour on Sark. After a particularly awful crossing, my priest walked up the steep concrete steps on to the jetty to be met by one of the Sark Carriers. First in line was Cyril

Wackley with his horse and cart. One mile up the steep harbour hill to Carrefour, where the horses were rested and refreshed with hay and water; then another quarter-mile up The Avenue to what the priest assumed would be a grand house, visualising perhaps a minor member of the ruling classes. Instead, the poor man arrived, green around the gills, to find no Sarkese dignitaries but my parents, brothers and our donkey Judy waiting to greet him. After performing an extremely grumpy baptism, he hoisted himself back on to the cart to begin his return journey.

Anyway, he did what he came to do and I was baptised Charmian Clare. As the changeable days wore on, my parents began to lose confidence in the name they'd chosen for me. They wondered what had possessed them to plump for a name with such a hard beginning, and one that neither even liked much. But their flirtation with the Shakespearean theme had already begun with Sebastian and Fabian and, by the time I arrived, they found it hard to stop. What seemed like a good idea at the time, three names ending with 'Ian', now just seemed silly. After a great deal of thought – Christabel, Fleur and Branch were all in the running – they finally settled for my more prosaic middle name. It took time for it to catch on, but eventually Charmian was given the cold shoulder and Clare was embraced with an equal measure of shyness and relief. In spite of this, I was only ever called Boo-Boo or darling, and on the rare occasions I was called Clare I knew I was in for it.

The rent for Le Chalet was fixed at eighty pounds a year for a ninety-year lease, but when my parents decided to return to London, they let it go. Money was always in short supply, and eighty pounds a year was an amount they could never rely on earning. Making money was one of those things other people seemed able to do, but was a virtual impossibility for my father, born without a solitary shrewd hair on his head. The largest amount of money he managed to make in his lifetime was the magnificent and unimaginable one hundred pounds, courtesy of Sir Kenneth Clarke, who bought several of Mervyn's drawings in one go. We lived on what he made by illustrating classics. His illustrations for *Alice in Wonderland, The Hunting of the Snark* and *The Rime of the Ancient Mariner* fed and clothed us.

Neither Mervyn nor Maeve could ever be accused of good business sense, and the only time a real money-spinner was handed to my father on a plate, he got it monumentally wrong. Commissioned to design the logo for Pan Books, the iconic black figure blowing his flute was created. Offered ten pounds on the spot or a percentage of every book sold, Mervyn, armed with advice from Graham Greene that the paperback book was just a temporary solution to the paper shortage, chose the money. Regret, luckily, was something neither of them went in for.

In 1950 we left Sark. My father needed to be in London where the commissions were and, after nearly four years of isolation from friends, galleries and bookshops, but with a real sense of nostalgia for what they were leaving behind, they packed their meagre possessions, left everything else (except the beloved kitchen table) and returned to London. It had been a fertile time, and a more thrilling adventure for my brothers than anyone could ever have imagined, and it was desperately hard to say goodbye. At nine months old, oblivious to the wrench they were all feeling, I blithely followed.

Trafalgar Studios Tribute

When I was three I began nursery school in Glebe Place, Chelsea, and my first clear memory is being collected by my father and hearing my first joke.

It was always winter then. Later on, after the age of ten, all memory is illuminated in arc light, but when I was three it was foggy and icy cold, and the empty London pavements made it possible to skip and run and jump in puddles with a freedom that was heavenly. I wore a beret and mittens, a scarf and corduroy trousers, and I held my father's hand as we walked along the almost deserted King's Road and into Hemming's Bakery for some hot chocolate and a Chelsea bun. 'We're in Chelsea, darling; we may as well have one of their buns,' he said. I thought it was funny, and from then on that sentence formed part of our daily conversation.

Augustus John's studio was close by and we might visit him, or stop off at Green & Stone, the art suppliers in the King's Road, to buy a tube of paint or some brushes, or ask prices of the canvases. They were usually too expensive, and something inside me stored away the almost, but not quite, audible sigh of disappointment, as my father charily replaced the taut and tempting canvas against the wall and picked up a shiny new tube of paint instead. On those occasions he made do with hardboard, a nasty and unsatisfactory substitute, or whitewashed a finished canvas and began again. Standing next to him, surrounded by brushes and easels, drawing pads and watercolour sets, left me with a feeling of absolute contentment and security. Names of paints stick in my mind, names that were both familiar and mysterious, and inextricably linked to him – burnt umber, Indian red, crimson lake, cobalt blue, rose madder. Those words, floating three foot above my head, landed in my subconscious and settled there.

Our studio, one of Trafalgar Studios, a purpose-built block in Manresa Road, was just across the road from my nursery school in Glebe Place. Once inside, the warmth hit me instantly, the beautiful warmth of the paraffin heater, and next the overwhelming smell of turps, a smell so evocative that sometimes I am tempted to have one quick sniff of the stuff just to recapture those pungent, happy days of my childhood. Dozens of differently shaped canvases, stacked against each other, leant against all four walls, and a yellow light poured through the gigantic, grimy windows that hid us from life outside. It was an enclosed world of such intense living, such intense creation, such intense security that I could have stayed in it forever, and been happy.

The key to the studio was attached to a string that had worn thin in the middle. It was frayed and coiled from being posted back and forth through the letter-box so many times a day and, as my father opened the vast double door, another smell filled my nostrils – newly baked fudge. Whether the making of fudge coincided with my arrival, or whether it would have been made daily anyway, I don't know, but I would be ushered into the huge studio of our neighbours, sat on a high stool with two or three pale, crumbly cubes cradled in my lap, and urged to tell the events of my school morning to an apparently captivated audience. Mrs Grimm, a massive woman with an oversized nose and flowing orange hair, would bundle me into her enormous bosom and kiss me passionately with the blood red mouth her cigarette had temporarily left, her kisses lingering in stale sweetness on my face. Mr Grimm, a large, round man with sparkling blue eyes, would put a protective arm around me, thrust his head back and laugh. With his colossal white beard and long wispy hair that trailed the neck of his blue artist's smock, I thought he was Father Christmas. He wore sandals, corduroy trousers and a black beret, and he smelt of tobacco and fudge. Our delight in each other's company was mutual. I liked nothing better than chattering to them about my day and, although I found the laughter that followed everything I said inscrutable, I sensed it wasn't meant to be unkind. Perhaps I went there so that Dad could get on with work. I always imagined they just wanted my company.

Back in our studio I lay on the floor and drew with the pencils and crayons that were kept there for me, or curled up on the huge, oddly comfortable, green armchair, with an Orlando or Babar picture book on my lap, pushing the stuffing back in with one hand and bending the wires poking through with the other so they didn't dig too much. My mother bought me colouring-in books but I could tell by the slant of my father's shoulders that he wasn't keen, and much preferred me drawing freehand. Despite the encouragement, I had absolutely no aptitude for drawing, much preferring to look at books and watch my father's face when he was painting – his forehead lined in concentration, a cigarette dangling from his lips, the smoke from his

44

Player's unfiltered curling round the room, filling it with a gorgeous, familiar smell. I watched him as he mixed the paints on his palette, as he walked backwards, stood two feet away from the painting, then moved in so close that his nose was almost touching the canvas. If I stayed silent, he stayed silent, but sometimes I wanted to interrupt his concentration, I wanted to be noticed. Then he took his cue from me, put his paintbrush down, looked me full-square in the face, and gave me one of the kisses I was always after.

Although I remember the studio well, we actually lived in a rented flat close by, in Embankment Gardens, a place so insignificant to my memory that it made no impression on me at all. But in 1953, on a whim, Maeve and Mervyn decided to leave Embankment Gardens and take up residence in The Grange, an absurdly unsuitable Georgian house in Smarden, Kent. It was an elegant pile, with orchards, gables and a great sense of itself, a house built for people with means and an understanding of the country-side. But my parents were never country folk and the English countryside wasn't the same thing as the island living they had become used to. To be surrounded by sea could be claustrophobic and lonely, but here they felt alien and homesick for London. Their dream of giving their offspring a childhood away from the city was short-lived and, before long, we moved back to Chelsea. My mother's explanation for leaving Smarden was of when the woman in a neighbouring house, popping round for advice on her husband's birthday present, replied to Maeve's 'What about a book?' with 'Oh no, he's already got one.'

While still living in Kent, we kept on the studio, and I often stayed the night there. Sometimes it was all five of us; sometimes it was just Dad and me. Making my bed couldn't

45

have been easier. Two similar-sized canvases would be propped against each other like vast playing cards, not toppling, but rigid as a priest's hands. Inside the canvases, still smelling of paint and occasionally still wet, it was warm and dark. A blanket was draped over each end, the blankets and the weave of the tawny brown canvas shutting out most of the light. Sometimes the paintings faced me, and sometimes the pictures were placed wrong side in. In the dim glow I could study the backs of the wooden frames, the minute tacks, and the overlapping canvas cloth. I could examine the three pointed hats of the clowns, the wrinkled hands of the old Sarkese men, the cloudy sky of our island home, and the portraits of my mother. I drifted off to the curves and the lines and the contours of the thick paint my father used.

I was an Eskimo as I crawled in with my provisions for the night – blankets, torch, book, teddy bear and my 'bye bye'. This was a minuscule, square, unwashed piece of knitted blanket I wrapped around my nose, unwashed because if it *were* washed the smell of home vanished down the sink along with the water. Maeve and Mervyn, a foot away, sat beside each other on a threadbare sofa that had once graced the elegant and superior sitting room of my maternal grandparents, my mother knitting furiously and dextrously, working on the brightly coloured and abstractly designed jumpers, hats and socks she made for us all throughout our lives. Decades before their time, they were incredibly daring in their originality and verve. Often, Mervyn sat facing Maeve, a skein of wool taut around his raised hands, the single strand unfurling again and again around his bony fingers until it was wound into one large ball. If the dismal sky of the bomb-damaged London was

46

depressing, the furniture past its best and money hard to find, Maeve seemed determined that her family took it on kitted out in a rainbow of vivid colours. Dressed as colourfully as any West Indian family on their way to church, the reds and oranges, purples and greens, pinks and yellows were a kind of snub at the dinginess of our surroundings and a gesture of internal exuberance.

In my tent I could hear the muffled sounds of conversation and laughter between my parents, or the more strident noise of clinking glass and louder laughter when their friends dropped by. The meals Maeve cooked on the Baby Belling, the kedgeree, fish pie, toad in the hole and steak and kidney pudding, smelt delectable as I drifted off to sleep. Their friends living in or around Chelsea were all in the same boat. Nobody had any money, but most were beginning to forge some sort of creative impact on the world. Maeve and Mervyn were convivial hosts, and friends could be sure of a warm atmosphere and a hot meal at the studio. Everyone passed through, and I dropped off to the voices of many of the artists and writers of the day – Augustus John, John Minton, Rodney Ackland, Matthew Smith, Stevie Smith, Graham Greene, Kathleen Raine and Laurie Lee among so many others. In Dylan Thomas's case the studio became a home from home, somewhere to stay when the rows with Caitlin became unbearable or, worse, when his DTs had my parents nursing him through his tremors and terrifying hallucinations.

But just as easily it might have been a stranger that Mervyn had met and taken a liking to, someone he'd brought home to sit for him, or a woman with 'particularly good cheekbones' who might model for future illustrations. Keen on strangers, and empathetic by nature, his Christmas

Eves were spent under the arches at Waterloo. Arriving with his army greatcoat stuffed with cigarettes and quarter bottles of whisky to hand out to the tramps, Maeve would find herself an hour or two later laying an extra place. Mervyn, looking no more well-fed than the people he met, would have patronised no one. There had always been something he didn't like about the exclusivity of Christmas, making people without the luxury of family and friends feel even more isolated than ever.

Now, when it's too late for recollections, I wish I'd asked more about these people when I had the chance. In all the conversations I had with my mother over the thirty-three years I knew her, I never did. In passing, she told me a little, alluded to magical times in Soho, spoke of lively conversations in the Café Royal, of candlelit dinners in the Blue Cockatoo by the river. There weren't many anecdotes, but there were one or two – such as the occasion Graham Greene brought a loaded pistol to the studio and suggested a game of Russian roulette after enjoying an opium-filled pipe, or the time he and Mervyn held a party for everyone they could find with a name associated with bottoms. Giggling over the telephone directory, Mr and Mrs Bott, Botts, Bottomley and Botolph were invited to a Mystery Evening at some unknown venue where Graham and Mervyn mingled with the guests, observing the gasps of excitement as the coincidences of names tittered around them.

Gormenghast in Miniature

In 1954, when I was four, we moved from Chelsea to a house in the suburbs, left to Mervyn by Doc. For the next seven years we all rattled around in a huge Victorian eyesore made for family life, with large, freezing rooms of a multitude of sizes and atmospheres, an enormous (by Chelsea standards) square lawn, and two perfectly adequate Catholic schools within walking distance for my brothers and me. I loved the reassuring feel of the suburbs, my brothers were ambivalent and my parents hated it. They loved the house, they just hated where it was. When my grandparents had returned from China, it had been to this house, in green and leafy Surrey. When we moved to Wallington, what had once been open countryside was now strangled by rows of identical semi-detached houses, with one colourless high street and a railway station my parents used for a quick exit. Everyone appreciated the space – my parents could have their own studios, we could have our own rooms – but again it wasn't where Maeve and Mervyn's friends were. Mervyn, now teaching at the Central School of Art, became a reluctant commuter, and the mysteriously exciting phrase 'going up to town' became a familiar and often used expression.

Number 55 Woodcote Road was a plain old girl, a red-bricked folly with turrets and hidden rooms and an underground bomb shelter. It was sturdy and sensible and things worked in it but, more importantly, it had a sympathetic feel. Like Gormenghast in miniature, there was a room for every mood, and bells, left over from its Victorian childhood, that peeled around the house, shrill enough to have us all evacuating our particular corner. The bell would summon Mervyn from his study or studio, Sebastian from the music room where he sat hunched over his Premier drum kit, practising his mama-dada double-stroke rolls, and Fabian from the attic studio where he painted. On one slanted wall, in gigantic, black, block capitals he had scrawled 'I LOVE VINCENT'. I didn't know who Vincent was until Fabian informed me that he was a Dutch painter. I would be hidden, attempting to locate some warmth in one of the many frozen rooms. With a blanket tucked tightly round me I lay upside down on the same un-reupholstered chair I had curled up in at the studio, engrossed in *The Saturday Book* or *The Yellow Book* or the gigantic *Verve*. I would examine the *National Geographic* in rapt fascination, gawping at the women with sausage-shaped bosoms, astonished at the transformation from the young girls' bosoms in the photographs into these peculiar shapes, dreading my eventual metamorphosis. I stared at men with perfectly paired, gigantic holes pierced through extended ear lobes, at fierce pygmies with spears and loincloths, at natives with bones pushed through their noses and at plate-lipped men and women whom, my mother, looking over my shoulder, had once casually remarked, some people found very attractive.

Abandoning whatever we were absorbed in, we gathered

in the kitchen for the breakfast, lunch or supper Mum had prepared for us. Josh White, Sarah Vaughan, Fats Waller, Leadbelly, Fats Domino, Frank Sinatra's 'Songs for Swingin' Lovers', Billie Holiday's 'Songs for Distingué Lovers', fiery flamenco music or the melodious voice of Amalia Rodriguez and her passionate love songs belted out from the gramophone. If it wasn't the bell being rung, it would be my father calling for my mother – 'Maeve?' . . . 'Maevie?' . . . 'Ma-veee?' – his voice echoing round the house, increasingly anxious, until at last she was located, and he could carry on with his work, some intricate cross-hatching or a poem, content in the knowledge she was nearby and utterly fundamental to his work. That clarion cry followed us to our next house and to all the hospitals he found himself living in a few years later.

Maeve Maeve Maeve Maeve Maeve
Sweetheart. Little plum-cake. Little daisy-chain, Clare's Mother. Darling sweetheart and companion of all our ups and downs, I adore you. Today is all sun and showers – better than yesterday, a fitful day – rather exciting with huge cloud-masses building up into the air and El Greco skies and odd Byzantine lighting. Nature must have been to Spain. Perhaps the wind was introduced to Greco and the trees to Goya in the days of long ago.
Whimsy?

I went 'up to town' too. Every Christmas from the age of four or five I would be taken to London and left at a party given by Lady Moray, a former student of my father's, who went on to become a wonderful friend to my parents. She wrote:

51

I think it was in 1935 that I first met Mervyn at the school in Westminster when I was enrolled as a complete beginner in the life drawing class and he was one of the teachers. Looking back on it now, it seems certain that Mervyn had a real gift for teaching, combining a passionate enthusiasm for his subject with an extremely sensitive consideration for the feelings of his pupils. He was patient, incredibly generous of his time and attention, and never was I made to feel that my standard of talent was wanting.

How lucky I was to have been one of those to profit from his teaching. As well as being my instructor at the school, Mervyn taught me, by visits to art exhibitions and galleries, so much about drawing and painting. Through knowing Mervyn, therefore, my eyes were opened to another world and this made all the difference to my pleasure and happiness for the rest of my life, for which I shall always be grateful. This took place in spite of the difference in our ages and the sort of lives that we led and was entirely due to Mervyn's total unawareness of and complete disinterest in any material values whatsoever.

I would be collected promptly by a uniformed chauffeur. 'I have been sent by the Countess of Moray to collect Clare for Her Ladyship's party,' he announced. The party, held in an immense flat in Hans Place, was filled with extraordinarily self-assured and smart little girls, and the new dress that was made for me especially every year, looking so pretty before I left for the event, always seemed rather plain in comparison to the expensively frilled and shiny satin of the other girls. Waiting for the postman to deliver the tantalising brown parcel for Miss Clare Peake was one of the most thrilling events of my year. My name and address would be written and underlined in a spidery and shaky scrawl by Mrs Peach, an ancient dressmaker we had made friends with in Smarden. As I tugged at the always too tightly bound string and ripped the parcel apart, a crumpled new dress came tumbling out in need of a vigorous shake. This yearly ritual climaxed in the careful placing of my beautiful new dress on a wooden hanger. Facing my bed, the light from the hall seeped under my door to show me its full beauty in silhouette. But it was invariably understated, stylish and smart, made from velvet, or purple and green shot silk, the kind of dress a French girl might wear. Maeve, loving simplicity and clean lines herself, never really came to terms with my adoration of frills and ruffles, so that my dresses were the antithesis of flounce and the very stuff of *Madeline*.

But two things that would have ensured my party went with a swing remained infuriatingly elusive, though I hankered after them with a remarkable lust. The curls and dimples that tempted me with their femininity had proved to be impossible to achieve despite earlier attempts. Yet I begged my mother to persevere. I vaguely understood her reticence when it came to dimples, but her inability to put a few curls in my hair perplexed me. What I didn't know about until much later was her utter loathing for preening or self-conscious children, so there was never much uniformity, or any enthusiasm, in her efforts. The strips of torn sheets and pipe cleaners were wound around my hair in a curious mixture of half-heartedness and painstaking solemnity, and I was acutely aware of her boredom in attempting to transform her daughter into a prissy 'little lady'. In the morning, with still a glimmer of hope that ringlets might spring jauntily from my scalp, I pulled at the torn rags and bent pipe cleaners with renewed optimism, only to find yet again that after twenty minutes my naturally dead straight hair had returned and flopped over my face with not so much as the memory of a wave. My arms still ached from poking two pencils at a ninety-degree angle in my cheeks, until I finally fell asleep and awoke in the morning to find two pink indents still smarting from a wretched and fruitless search for dimples. To go with my party dress I would be given a crisp paper bag stuffed to the rim with ribbons. Cut with pinking shears to prevent fraying, the identical lengths of tartans and ginghams, polka-dots and stripes would guarantee that at least my plaits and pony-tails would be dressed to perfection.

I was extremely shy with strangers, so felt a mixture of excitement and dread for this annual party. As we sat cross-legged on the silk rugs and watched the magicians and conjurers perform for us, then lined up one by one to have our photograph professionally taken in a formal and elegantly carpeted room, I felt strangely alone. There was a ritual to it all that I wasn't used to, and an innate self-confidence displayed by these rich, coiffed and supremely certain children. I shrank into myself and my throat hurt as I held in the tears that were longing to burst from my eyes. Lady Moray couldn't have been kinder or more welcoming, and it wasn't my dress, or even the other girls; it was a feeling of not quite belonging, of not understanding the rules of this very different world. It all felt so alien and I longed to go back to the warmth and simplicity of home.

Although my mind and body were able to do unrestrained cartwheels in a house where the furniture was ancient, the walls covered in murals or mould, the sheets wafer thin, the chairs disfigured by body shapes and the windows naked, everything around me was astonishingly organised and extremely tidy. Mealtimes and bedtime were set at conventional hours, brushing of teeth and night-time stories were of paramount importance, manners were taught and rotas were set. It was just the laughter and sea of love I was marooned in that was unconventional in its lavish generosity.

Our house was so huge I thought the world began and ended in it – twenty differently shaped rooms, some with eaves, some with skylights, some minuscule, some huge, all with cobwebs. Rooms where books lined shelves from floor to ceiling, where paintings covered every inch of available wall, a minute space between each one so that shamed spaces, where plaster had crumbled off, were alive with colour. Stuffed birds perched on knotty, tube-shaped logs and ranged in size from thrush to eagle. On a whim, my father had bought them for Fabian, as a job lot from Maidstone Museum, at a moment in his life when he felt his and Fabian's existence would not be complete without them. Vases of sweet peas balanced precariously on whale vertebrae, three of which had been salvaged from a beached whale during Mervyn's two-year sojourn in Sark as a young man. Enormous turquoise and rust-coloured plaster dragons brought home from China guarded the fireplace, a lay figure, dressed in an orange Chanel suit and clasping a pink cigarette, sat on a wicker chair and could be contorted to any position we felt like putting her in. She sat patiently, legs splayed, back curved, neglected and forgotten until someone remembered to use her as a model.

The rooms were used for the endless rounds of sardines, hide-and-seek and blind man's buff that we played with our friends. People came to visit, children stayed, we put on plays, we rode bikes, we erected tents and one freezing winter Mervyn built us an igloo. He packed large oblong blocks into perfectly shaped bricks and fixed an unused pane of glass in the back, from where a painted Eskimo peered out at us. It was warm enough to sleep inside, and easy to imagine we were living in a house in the North Pole and not in the garden of a house a few dreary miles from Croydon. We had relay races and treasure hunts, and grown-ups wandered around the house or sat on striped deck chairs in the garden, talking to Mervyn and Maeve. They sipped fresh lemonade with sprigs of mint on top, still as Ophelia, or drank the mysteriously named 'Gin and It'. They were a disparate bunch – poets and painters mingled with neigh-bours and relatives, the ordinary and the extraordinary. Cranking up the wind-up gramophone, we lolled on the green and brown patchy lawn, listening to the same 78 rpm records over and over again. I remember those long summer nights, and how, when everyone had gone, I could really let my hair down and dance around the garden, singing along to my favourite songs, 'If I Didn't Care' and 'Java Jive' by the Inkspots, 'I'm Going to Sit Right Down and Write Myself a Letter' by Fats Waller, 'Blueberry Hill' by Fats Domino, 'A Room with a View' and 'The Party's Over Now' by Noël Coward. His songs felt like home, those two in particular giving me a funny feeling in my heart, a bitter-sweet nostalgia I was too young to recognise, but made me want to weep.

As bedtime stories were such an integral part of family life, they were told whether I was on my own or had a friend to stay. They followed a reassuring pattern. Dad would knock at the door, I would bid him enter and he'd come in smiling and carrying a tray covered with snacks he'd rustled up in the kitchen and a mug of Horlicks or Ovaltine. If my friend Helen stayed the night, we'd eat and drink in silence, waiting for our story to begin. They were always different, and you only had to close your eyes to be transported to a black sea, alive with swashbucklers, planks and dreadful Cornish accents (a mimic, my father was not), a magic land where roaming fairies hid within tulip petals, or a deserted moor where kilted men played the bagpipes to dancing elves. On the more intimate occasions when I was by myself, my father lay down with me, my sleepy head cradled in the hollow of his bony shoulder as he unhurriedly continued with our progressing story of Tommy Titmouse and his courageous exploits in the jungles of Madagascar. Or he invented a nonsense poem. I only had to give him a first line, 'My best friend is awfully funny' or 'I hate getting up in the morning', for a poem to materialise.

He read me Lewis Carroll, Ogden Nash, Hilaire Belloc, A. A. Milne and Beatrix Potter, but there was one book he refused to read – *Struwwelpeter*. Every night I requested it, and every night he said no. He had witnessed the consequences of the times he had said yes. But the book had such a powerfully seductive appeal that I waited until he left the room, pulled my brother's copy from beneath my mattress, threw the blankets over my head, and switched on my torch to illuminate the book's unequivocal message to naughty children. With a paralysing fear of the punishments awaiting me if I didn't follow *Struwwelpeter*'s cautionary tales to the letter, I never played with matches and I always drank my soup but, however hard I tried, it was impossible not to suck my thumb. So I fell asleep in a state of acute terror, waiting for the 'great tall tailor – the red-legg'd scissor man' to creep into my bedroom and lop off my thumbs. Although they were still attached to my hand in the morning, I knew it was only a matter of time.

My mother's family visited often. She came from a great octopus of a tribe. There were so many aunts, uncles and cousins that, to this day, there are countless relatives I've never met. Those I did know were all devout Roman Catholics, and all with accents you could shear a sheep with. They had no interest whatsoever in the 'arts' but an inordinate interest in musicals and bridge, neither of which interested my parents particularly. Everyone was very fond of each other, but I sometimes felt, perhaps unfairly, that my parents were viewed as charming eccentrics, foreigners to that land unimaginative people always refer to so glowingly as 'the real world' – a world my parents were actually on first-name terms with. Confusingly at odds with what they would have seen as the artistic temperament was Maeve's extraordinary elegance, such a rarity in England that it was always remarked upon. She had few clothes, but she wore them well and would have looked far more at home walking down the Champs Elysées than Wallington high street. So the nephews were fascinated by her, and the nieces wanted to be like her. I understood – so did I. There were no sandals or hairy toes in our house – well, not on Maeve anyhow.

Mervyn's family, on the other hand, was small. There was just his one brother Lonnie, an utterly adorable big bear of a man, born without a single creative bone in his body and as lacking in artistic dexterity as Mervyn was in Lonnie's excellent business brain. A partner at Pricewaterhouse, and the chairman of Raffles Hotel in Singapore, he had the same smell and sweetly affectionate qualities as my father. Lonnie and Mervyn had both inherited Doc's acutely sensitive nature and could blub at the drop of a hat, yet when it came to the really difficult things in life, all three were, outwardly, masters of the stiff upper lip and English restraint. Lonnie, a tall and powerfully built man with the same deep-set eyes, gentle voice and full mouth as Mervyn, had been captured by the Japanese, and had spent the next four-and-a-half years in Changi Jail, the notoriously brutal prisoner of war camp. Like so many others, after the war was over he found it impossible to talk of his experiences to anyone, even those closest to him.

One ordinary day soon after the end of the war, Lonnie arrived unexpectedly at the studio. Maeve didn't recognise the emaciated man being helped to the door by a tearful taxi driver, who refused the fare in a never-to-be-forgotten act of kindness. Lonnie's rugby physique had shrivelled to a skeletal six stone. His wife and children were in Canada, so he had come to his brother Mervyn's. He slept and he ate. A diet of rice, day after day, year after year, had him dreaming of nothing more exotic than the luxury of bread and butter.

Both brothers were profoundly affected by their war-time experiences, and both spoke to no one about what they had witnessed. While Lonnie kept his thoughts close to his chest, at least Mervyn could find release in drawing and poetry. Though in everyday life Lonnie and Mervyn had heads filled with thoughts disparate in the extreme, they shared a fanatical love of cricket. They could talk endlessly of scores and runs and wickets and innings, and they could talk of China.

Long after my father died, and after the funeral of Lonnie's Canadian wife, Ruth, we all wandered back from the graveyard in Burpham, Sussex (where both my parents are buried) to his beautiful thatched cottage, where Doc and Bessie had once lived, for that strange little party that occurs after someone dies. Noticing Lonnie had disappeared, I tapped on his bedroom door and found him perched on the edge of their bed, staring into the distance. As I walked into their room he held his arms out to me like a child, sobbed quietly into my bosom, gave a deep, involuntary sigh and murmured, 'Ooh, that's better,' and I held on to him because I loved him, but also because if I inhaled deeply enough I could smell my father.

I never knew any of my grandparents, and I am ashamed to say that, growing up, I never gave a thought to any of them. I wasn't starved of an older perspective, though. My elderly godmother, Laura, had been a missionary nurse in the hospital in Tientsin, and had assisted Doc in delivering Mervyn all those years before. An important bond was forged between my family and Laura, and when she returned to England in 1939 she became a lifelong family friend. She retired to Buckinghamshire, but every so often came up to London to see friends, and stayed at the Goring Hotel, close to Victoria Station, where I went to visit her. These meetings were always just between the two of us. Laura would be waiting for me in the hotel lounge and, after an affectionate greeting, I would be overpowered by the three-tiered scent of loose face powder, eau de cologne and mothballs on her elaborately whitened skin. I would join her for tea and sponge cake, and tiny triangular sandwiches covered in cress and filled with chicken and ham pastes and lurking slices of cucumber, which I stuffed into my pocket when she wasn't looking.

After tea we rumbled slowly upwards in the minute, beeswax-smelling lift to the austere and joyless room she always stayed in. Sitting me down on her rigid bed, hardened by the mysterious plank of wood the staff placed under her mattress especially for her, she presented me with the gift she had brought with her. Wrapped in crisp tissue paper, it was always Chinese, and invariably something that had belonged to her. A jade bracelet, brittle and beautifully mottled in cloudy greens and whites, wrapped in layers of apricot cloths and squeezed into a square straw case; a velvet choker with a transparent locket containing a switch of her snow-white hair; a silver ring carved in Chinese letters; a plate patterned with painted dragons; or perhaps a Chinese puzzle.

These gifts would be given with enormous ceremony, a story linked to each, and a second story illustrating my place in China via Mervyn's birth. For a long time I imagined I had Chinese blood, assuming that if Dad had been born in China he must be Chinese, confused by the intricacies and complexities of the whereabouts of birth. I liked the idea, and periodically gazed in the mirror to see if my eyes had changed shape. Laura told me of her life as a missionary, and of Mervyn as a little boy. Of his adventures in Tientsin, his drawing, his marvelling at the goose-egg size of the chalky gallstone that Doc removed from a tiny Chinaman, and that I still have.

She hinted at a solitary life without a husband or children and, to my astonishment, her contentment without either. She had thick white hair worn in a bun, held up with a jade or ivory comb. She wore brightly coloured silk jackets and ornate dangling earrings, and she was terribly old. I was mesmerised by her hands. They were stark white and covered with huge gingery coloured freckles the size of a sixpence, the skin so thin and transparent I could almost see

61

the bones, the veins making maps that I imagined led her back to China. She took her role as my godmother extremely seriously, and I felt utterly adored by her, from the moment her eyes lit up as I entered the lobby of the Goring to the loving cry of 'Boo-Boo' when she saw me. Her mandarin-collared jackets decorated with hand-painted dragons, straw hats and black silk trousers ending two inches above her ankle made her appearance incongruous and very glamorous amid the dreariness of the bowler-hatted, pin-striped-suited workers of post-war Victoria.

The soulless Victoria became part of the very stuff of my childhood. The cartoon cinema was next to the station and Dad and I often made the bleak and uninteresting train journey from Surrey to see each new film as it appeared. We peered out of the carriage's dirty windows at the grimy rooftops as smoke billowed from chimneys, and at greyed sheets blowing in the wind in inner London gardens. Mervyn drew on the pad he kept with him, or sketched on a deconstructed cigarette packet, the cigarettes ejected and housed in his pocket until later. There was always a head he thought interesting enough to draw, a wrinkled ear he felt compelled to jot on paper, a beautiful jaw line aching to be recorded. Unknowingly, he taught me how to look, and our eyes met as we registered the pug nose or the beautiful neck of our fellow passenger. He noticed everything; there wasn't an eyelid, a chin, a walk, a stance, a shape of head he didn't see in a glance, and he noticed my nose. He said I had a good nose – a Grecian nose.

I took my piece of blanket, my 'bye bye', with me everywhere, and it was returning home from one of these outings that I left it behind on a bus. Finding it impossible to sleep without it, I lay in bed, becoming more and more agitated. Dad kissed me goodnight, promising if I went to sleep without a fuss, it would be with me when I woke in the morning. I drifted off and, just as he said, when I woke, there it was in my hand. Taking the next train back to London, he had got down on his hands and knees and searched every bus in Victoria's bus depot until he finally found the six-inch-square, smelly, moth-eaten piece of wool. To the astonishment of the bus conductors he held it up in triumph and without feeling the need for explanation made his way back home.

In 1956, before everything changed, Dad took me to see John Ford's *The Searchers*. I was six and it was the first adult film I'd seen, and the outing was meant as a treat. Instead it petrified me, leaving me with nightmares that lasted for weeks. It filled me with a prescient doom, as though there were a part of me that was waiting for something to go wrong, to shatter this happiness in which I felt myself enveloped. I'd never seen tears and drama in such abundance; I'd never seen such anger in men before. I identified with Debbie Edwards, played by Natalie Wood, and Dad became Ethan Edwards, Debbie's uncle, played by John Wayne (a more improbable comparison would be hard to find) who searches for the next five years for his vanished niece. Squinting through my fingers, I convinced myself there was a possibility that I, too, could be captured.

I imagined Dad searching for me for years. I knew he'd search forever, that he'd never abandon me, but I worried that when we were finally reunited I would have altered so much it would be impossible for him to recognise me. I visualised him ripping open the tepee, penetrating my eyes for the smallest glimmer of recognition, examining the ochre lines on my face, and then leaving without knowing I was

63

his daughter. Somehow all this emphasis on tomahawks, stamping feet, arrows, John Wayne and loss jumbled together so that images disturbed my sleep and left me feeling insecure for the first time in my life.

I began to experience nightmares just as Fabian had done when he was small. Fabian's involved a lion that sat on its haunches and peered at him threateningly through his bedroom window. The lion's inevitable pounce halted only when Mervyn came into the fray. He rushed at the window and the exhausting battle ceased when the defeated lion was pushed off the ledge, falling twenty feet and scurrying away forever into the black night, his long tail clasped firmly between his legs.

My nightmare was set in a suburban playground and involved recurring visits from an older girl on a swing. She had thick black plaits tied with a red ribbon and, although she looked familiar, I was never able to place her. Her pinched and cloudy face was spiteful, and her close-set eyes crinkled with malevolence as she swung higher and higher. Her upturned feet missed my head by inches, her right foot scraping the ground beneath her to accelerate, as her raucous and mocking cackle became more and more hysterical. I couldn't move, I couldn't run away and I woke myself up on several occasions, sometimes screaming, sometimes standing by the side of my bed as if glued to the concrete. My restlessness had one or other of my parents coming to my room to reassure me that, although it was nasty, it was just a nightmare. But when her visits became more frequent, Dad decided it was time to take control. One night he burst into my room and I woke to find him dragging the girl off the swing and clutching her by her plaits. His eyes blazed as he warned her that this was to be the last visit she ever made.

I was astonished by it all, his voice, his strength, his fury, but mainly his absolute belief in the power of this girl. She never returned, and I fell asleep that night, and every night after that, without a care in the world.

Maeve and Mervyn's love of children and real understanding of what made them tick made our house the place other children wanted to be. It was a place where being a child and doing what children do wasn't going to land you in trouble, somewhere of gaiety and non-conformity, where childhood in all its idiosyncrasy was not viewed as something to be got through, but the template for everything. My birthday parties were wonderful occasions. To get us in the mood they began with a hokey-cokey. Dad, leading the way as squealing children held on to each other's waists, sped down the garden, into the shrubbery, up the stairs, through the house and into the attic. His arms and legs contorted into shapes we copied, and we eventually tripped and fell on top of each other in a pile of screaming, hysterical girls. There were sing-alongs at the piano with Maeve, and drawing lessons with Mervyn, the usual pass the parcel, musical statues, musical chairs, pin the tail on the donkey, and then an elaborate tea in the garden. Maeve's gingerbread men wore striped trousers and bow ties, and her gingerbread girls wore full dresses and lipstick. Sandwiches were cut into animal shapes and jellies became castles. As the action-packed party drew to a close, a queue began to form as one by one the children sat for the portrait Mervyn would do of each of them as an extra going-away present.

Jealousy and How it Makes You Feel

We were all settled in our local schools by now, and it was usually Dad who picked me up in the afternoon. It was there that it first became clear to me that the effect he had on the women we met was rather unusual. Teachers and parents changed around him. They became flirtatious and silly and, all of a sudden, I became a girl of consequence. They flattered me in a way I sensed was for his benefit and, looking back, I'm sure he saw it, too. I found it curious and perplexing. The response I saw came from women of every shape and size, the plain and the beautiful, the brilliant and the stupid. As Michael Moorcock put it: 'Women certainly fell in love with his sheer beauty. And then with his charm. And then with his wit. And then they were lost.' I ,of course, didn't see him in those terms. If he'd been a short, stout, balding fellow with the same innards, my feeling towards him would have been exactly the same.

He may have been unaware of his magnetism, or perhaps he had just become used to this response. All I knew was that, from my position at the end of Dad's hand, they all reacted in the same way. They kept him talking as though a piece of his glamour might rub off on them but, as we walked off together, I felt so connected to him that, instead of feeling superfluous on these occasions, I instinctively understood my weight. Maeve had the same effect on men, and both of them sailed through life oblivious to the fact that this wasn't usual, that eyes lighting up when you said hello didn't happen to everyone. Their dual attractiveness to the opposite sex was naturally never referred to but, on one occasion, I got a little closer to understanding from my mother's perspective what it was like to be married to a man whose looks and talent made him the object of other women's fantasies. Sailing down Park Lane on a double-decker bus one afternoon when I was ten or eleven, Maeve and I discussed Vivien Leigh. We'd been to see *Gone With the Wind* and were talking of her luminous beauty. Maeve told me of an evening when she and Mervyn and the Oliviers had gone to the theatre together. Miss Leigh was flirting with Mervyn a little too obviously and a little too disrespectfully for Maeve's liking. Feeling intensely jealous and extremely threatened, she narrowed her eyes until they were almost slits; green fire billowed from her nose, as she planted a look of venom on Vivien Leigh, a look that said, 'You go near my man and I'll kill you.' To my father's chagrin, sitting next to Vivien Leigh and oblivious to the exchange of looks, Miss Leigh suddenly gave her full attention to the play in progress.

Joan Greenwood's crush was a harder nut to crack. Unperturbed by his marital status, she would turn up at the studio, rap on the door and in her wonderfully seductive purr would whisper, 'I've come to see Mervyn,' brushing past Maeve as if she were the only fly in the ointment of their great passion. I felt oddly flattered that day. My mother didn't go in for personal revelations and it was invigorating to be told of something so real and adult, about the terribleness of jealousy and how it makes you feel.

I didn't distinguish between my parents, so the decision about which one to go to when I had a problem or a request was an arbitrary one. If I needed a costume for a school play, it usually ended up with Dad making it. My initial pride in these eccentric constructions was always tempered with more than a twinge of embarrassment when it came to dress rehearsals. At home, my costume seemed entirely obvious, but at school, as our ten green bottles prepared to line up (the brief being 'a green bottle'), nine similar, emerald-green crepe paper girls walked freely, head, arms and legs exposed, as I shuffled in – number seven, eyes squinting from slits knifed from the neck of an exquisite and elaborately painted absinthe bottle. It wasn't with any sense of one-upmanship that Dad made these things. He just couldn't have made a dreary costume if he'd tried and his personal philosophy that 'everything matters' was never more apt than on these occasions. Every inch of every costume was made with minute attention to detail.

'Who Killed Cock Robin?' the cry went up on another occasion and, as the murderous spiders and hens plodded on the stage, the narrator looked mysteriously at the audience. With narrowed eyes he scanned the stage as I, poor Cock Robin, a pathetically put upon, murdered, red apparition, circled the stage in a costume so magnificent in its colour and detail, it was no wonder their intentions were less than honourable. My less-than-starring role as an autumn leaf in another school play had the family looking and learning about the beauty of trees, as Dad sewed an array of fallen, rust, yellow and orange leaves on to a piece of gauze that covered my body and had dried up and crinkled for the second performance.

Even though 'things' bored my father, he knew a thing of beauty when he saw it. He liked to spoil people and he loved to treat my mother to strange and beautiful jewellery – an amethyst bracelet the size of a small new potato, earrings so ornate they jangled with cockiness and collided with her chin, two similar-sized stones he found on the beach and polished until they shone. He bored a perfect hole into each to fit the silver wire that would fit into her ear lobes. What interested him were the relics found on his travels. I found it all perfectly natural and became just as excited as he was when he emptied his pockets of his booty – a pair of glasses with a tangled-up frame and one lens missing, a large gentleman's hankie, a pair of false teeth or a lone shoe. We would have endless discussions about every item. In dozens of cases there were combs with three three-quarters of the teeth missing. I have no idea what he wanted with these things; they just interested him. Someone else might feel the same about a piece of Meissen.

One of the reasons I was so close to my father was that he was always there. He worked from home, so could be located at any time, and the ordinary chat one had in the course of a day was seamless and natural. There were no dispensations for the artist, no tiptoeing feet padded the floor, no indulgent silences or whispering voices made me uncomfortable in my own house. Able to interrupt at any time, my brothers and I were unaware that we were interrupting. We were the raw material for his illustrations. 'Stand just like that will you?' he would say as we posed on the spot, then ran off to continue whatever we were doing. He took his work, but not himself, seriously, and that was plain in everything I saw. Twenty-three of his own and twenty-four books illustrated for other people were published between 1939 and 1961, dozens of portraits and thousands upon thousands of drawings were produced. There wasn't a second when he wasn't working, yet he was as accessible as anyone else's father. This modest attitude generated its own respect. This lack of preciousness, mixed with gentle authority, had me loving nothing more than sitting quietly on his lap, watching as a drawing took shape, as a pencil was sharpened, as a shaken paintbrush magically clouded the transparent jam jar into one of rainbow-coloured turps. His fingers moved across a blank piece of paper as nimbly and gracefully as Fred Astaire's feet across a dance floor. A picture would appear from nowhere, and I would have been there from conception to birth.

The fact that my father didn't wear his genius on his sleeve might imply he wasn't serious-minded and consumed. The reverse was true. He was passionately consumed. His head was bursting; he just didn't let on. He was an artist to his fingertips, but his way of working appeared effortless. He wrote in bed with the blankets tucked tightly round him, or drew with his legs dangling over the side of a chair, smoking a pipe or cigarette, with Maeve reading him passages from his hero, Charles Dickens, or a chapter from *The Diary of a Nobody* or a poem by one of his favourite poets, Robert Frost.

Listen With Mother

Seasons are long in childhood, and winters never-ending. Time seemed real and didn't race by before you'd lived it. There was no central heating, and no fire lit in the daytime to escape the freezing temperature outside. Life was lived inside the house, and once in, that's where you stayed. By six o'clock we were huddled round the fire in a coal-black sitting room, telling ghost stories and watching the wood crackle over the scrunched-up news-paper, toasting crumpets at the end of a long devil's fork. My legs were covered in scars and scald marks from ambitiously hot, stone water bottles, kicked round the bed in a vain attempt at warming every spot. In the morning, I dreaded leaving my bed, plucking up the courage to take off my pyjamas and button the white liberty bodice to my navy-blue pleated school skirt. Times were austere. Doors were closed to keep the heat in, lights were switched off as you left a room, left-over food became tomorrow's supper. The war had made people careful and waste of any sort was discouraged. Ration books were being phased out, but temperance was not.

My parents were of the generation who washed every

nook and cranny of their bodies with a boiled flannel (I suspect my father's boiling was a little lacklustre in comparison with my mother's) and viewed a daily bath as an indulgence. They were mistrustful and frightened by any new addition to the house. Everything was used until it rotted. The interloper – a new tin-opener, fountain pen, sofa – had to pay its dues, because what they liked, what they felt comfortable with, were the desks, chairs, beds, tables, lamps and animals which they had built up some sort of relationship with. Some of this unspoken philosophy must have ingratiated itself into my psyche, because I remember the intense feeling of loneliness that a contemporary sofa from Tulley's gave me many years later. It replaced the one the five of us had sat on for years, at varying heights. Having no springs at one end, we went down in size like a picture of the story of evolution, except the other way round. I felt jealous on the old sofa's behalf, irritated by the chipper complacency of the new one's boastful springs, infuriated by its obvious lack of respect for any kind of proper history.

It was such a different time then, when anything new was cause for celebration. I knew nobody who lived any differently. One night we sat, my father, brothers and I, patiently waiting for Mum to give us a twirl in the new dress she had bought. Her eyes shone with excitement as she sashayed into the room. 'The Sack' by Christian Dior was the newest design from Paris, the most up-to-the-minute creation available, and anything more monstrously unflattering to a woman with the slightest hint of a curve you would be hard pressed to find. How they found the money to pay for it I'll never know, but what I do know is that it was a momentous occasion. We sat with our mouths open, unable to rally even a squeak.

'You hate it,' she said, her sad little voice breaking the heavy silence as she walked back out of the room, crushed by our reaction.

'No darling, it's just that you've got such a lovely figure and . . .' Dad called after her – too late, she'd gone. It hung, this sack-materialed, sack-coloured, shapeless sack, in her cupboard, in coventry, for the rest of its useless life. This story would mean nothing today, when buying a new dress is as common as buying a sprout, but back then it was something important, something to get excited about.

I was now a member of the Brownie fraternity, which I hated – the colour of the uniform, the lack of humour in Brown Owl, the prissy girls. But I had one great friend, Susan, a fellow pixie, whose parents owned a sweet shop quite close to where we lived which, to me, was the absolute pinnacle of luck and privileged living. Upstairs they had fluffy carpets and matching suites, but downstairs, and this was the best thing of all, we were allowed to 'play shops' with real money, real tills and real customers, making me the envy of lesser Brownies the length and breadth of Surrey. Whenever I stayed the night, her mother brought us treats in bed, which I've never forgotten. I was used to one Jamboree bag on a Friday night, so this was heaven, shameful in its opulence. Our individual trays were covered in sweets. The flying saucers, Spanish wood, dinosaur eggs, sherbet pips, aniseed balls, black jacks, bubble gum, fruit salads and gobstoppers were stacked on top of each other like a pyramid, and by their side was a tall glass of Tizer with a scoop of vanilla ice cream plopped in carelessly, so it fizzed like an experiment in a Jerry Lewis film. We woke in the morning with lipstick etched to our mouths, gum stuck to our hair and ice cream matted in our eyebrows, the

73

discarded wrappers slung to the floor with abandon. This was decadence on a grand scale, but what struck me more than the excess was the casualness with which our teeth were ignored. Being brainwashed daily at home on the importance of brushed teeth (although, curiously, too much washing was considered rather suburban), I crept into my friend's bathroom with my toothbrush at the ready, but her mother waylaid me at every turn. 'Oh, don't worry about that, leave it to the morning,' she said. Naturally, this small act of insurrection made it all the more exciting, but there was a slight frisson of malevolence, as though she got her kicks from imagining our teeth dropping out one by one by the time we were twelve.

One freezing night, while walking me home, Susan's mother told me a secret that my mother had sworn her to keep. Warning me not to 'tell on her', Susan's mum revealed that when I arrived home there would be a television. This was enormous news, as we were probably the only family in the northern hemisphere not to own one. The struggle to persuade Dad that there was any benefit at all in having a box we all stared at had been up-hill all the way. He had been violently opposed to the idea, fearing that ghost stories by the fireside would be replaced, that playing and reading would become obsolete, that talking to people's preoccupied profiles would become the norm.

As I walked up the drive, the imposing house was in silhouette. Drawing closer, through a chink in the sitting-room curtains, I could just make out a flickering screen and a keyed-up mother awaiting my return. It was all so thrilling, even more so than when Dad took us on outings in our new (to us) Humber Hawk. A drive to the country would involve many games of I spy, sing-alongs and the search for that ghastly and thankfully rare deviant, the man with a beard and no moustache. Fabian referred to those people as 'a thousand lashes', a term that mystified me until he explained that that was what he would like to give them.

Although these outings were fun, television was a much safer alternative. Mervyn was a terrible driver, being far more occupied with the shape of the noses he passed on the way than what was happening on the road. Picking me up from school one afternoon in our former beloved Land Rover, he forgot to shut my door properly and, being lost in thought, or having spotted a particularly feeble chin, he failed to notice I'd fallen out. He arrived home with the nagging sensation that he'd forgotten something. Luckily for both of us, someone had rescued me half a mile down the road. The next thing I remember is lying in my parents' bed, three knitted brows peering down at me, a long, thin torch searching each eyeball, a hankie daubed with smelling salts latched to my nose, and my wrist being picked up and dropped on the sheet like a dead haddock. The doctor spoke with abnormal slowness into my face. His breath smelt of mints.

'What – is – your – name?' he said.

'Clare,' I replied.

'Good, good!' he said. 'Where – do – you – live – Clare?'

'At – home,' I answered.

'Is she going to be all right?' Maeve asked in a voice of just the right speed. Mervyn stared down at me, his head bowed low with shame, my mother's eyes fixed on him with unconcealed fury.

'Yes, she'll be fine. She's just mildly concussed,' the doctor answered.

I had never seen my mother so angry.

That winter I walked to school in the dark and I walked home in the dark. Racing into the sitting room, I stumbled over chairs and sofas, feeling my way in a drawn-curtained, unlit room, to locate the television. I switched it on and waited for the endless warming-up of the twelve-inch black and white Ferguson to show me *Bill and Ben*, *Andy Pandy* and *The Woodentops*.

One day my school was given the afternoon off to watch Mervyn demonstrate some simple ways of drawing on a live children's BBC television programme. Maeve came to collect me, and we walked arm-in-arm through the dense and impenetrable pea-soup that made it impossible to see a foot in front of us, our mouths covered by woollen scarves to prevent the smog seeping into our lungs, while the tips of trilby-hatted men's cigarettes lit the way. Sick with nerves, we built a fire and sat silently in the coal-black sitting room, waiting, it seemed forever, for Dad to talk to us through a minute screen that he occupied with a calm authority.

Like most children, what I liked was routine. It made me feel secure and my life followed a pattern that suited me. After school and tea, a meal in itself, Mum and I trooped off to the music room where I curled up on her lap and waited for *Listen With Mother* to begin. After it was finished the wireless was turned off and she began to play the piano, as I warmed up for my dances à la Isadora Duncan. The music shifted swiftly, from tranquil to threatening, from urgent back to melodious as I invented scenes and situations for my imaginary characters to inhabit. I became trance-like and oblivious to my mother, as I spun and twirled to the rhythm of her energetic, willing, but slightly leaden piano.

This dance class of one was followed by our dual singing from Walter Crane's *The Baby's Opera, A Book of Old Rhymes With New Dresses* propped on the black upright brought home from China. I stood behind her as she put on a bravura performance, somehow managing to appear engrossed in the stagnant repetition of the day before, and the days before that. 'Oranges and Lemons', 'Lavender's Blue', 'Ding Dong Bell', 'Old King Cole', 'Ring a Ring a Roses', 'Hickory Dickory Dock', 'I Saw Three Ships' and 'The Grand Old Duke of York' – these songs, and the marching up and down the chilly room like a soldier, are engraved on my memory. Limpet-like, they stay with me.

Bath times were also an occasion to let rip, but then it was my mother who sang to me, and I joined in the chorus. As neither of us had a voice to write home about, our enjoyment was unfettered by vanity. A strict rotation of songs had been arrived at; beginning with 'Daisy Daisy', 'How Much is That Doggy in the Window?' and 'Mama's Little Baby Loves Shortenin', Shortenin'', she limbered up for her penultimate offering – her particular favourite, 'I Can't Give You Anything But Love'. It infused the steamy bathroom with husky-voiced emotion, as every word was relished to the hilt. Finally, the denouement, the unchanging and softly sung finale – 'When I was just a little girl, I asked my mother, what will I be? Will I be pretty? Will I be rich? Here's what she said to me. Que sera sera. Whatever will be, will be. The future's not ours to see. Que sera sera. What will be, will be.'

I was enormously interested in being pretty, and just as disinterested in being rich, and as Maeve sat on the lavatory seat to mix the hot and cold water from the rusty taps into a heavy saucepan, and then sloshed it in torrents over my head a dozen times until my hair squeaked, we pondered this question. As I looked up at her for the answer it was always in the affirmative. 'Not just pretty, darling. Beautiful.'

The World Turns Upside Down

Then one morning everything changed. Until that day, my first seven years had been notched up without the merest hint of a cloud. I was Daddy's girl, the girl waylaid on the stairs and squinted at like a stranger. 'Oh my goodness, who is this angel? Could it be my daughter? Could I be that lucky?' Or, 'What perfect timing, sweetie. I was feeling a bit lonely, come and sit on my lap, tell me what you think of this drawing, this painting, this poem.' By lunchtime, life had altered and repetition was a thing of the past. It took less than twenty-four hours for my father to forget who I was, or so it felt.

Mervyn had written a play called *The Wit to Woo*. It had taken years to be staged, the script having done the rounds of the British theatre establishment. The Oliviers, Peter Hall and Michael Codron were all interested, and enthusiastic letters had travelled back and forth for a year or so. At last, in 1957, it was to be produced at the Arts Theatre, but Maeve was apprehensive. The theatre was such a different world, far removed from the solitary world of writing and painting, and perhaps a cold place for the inexperienced. The play, Maeve said, was 'like a boulder rushing downhill. Nothing could stop it. It seemed to carry a sense of doom in it. There were too many people involved in it – whereas in a book, a painting, a poem, you are only answerable to yourself.'

For some reason, Mervyn had pinned his hopes for a better future on the play's success, and had an idea that if in the areas he was most confident he found it impossible to make any kind of living, maybe writing a play would be the answer. He was optimistic by nature, but not unnaturally so, yet his hopes for a successful outcome were uncharacteristically high. I was sitting at the kitchen table on the evening the play was finished. He suddenly emerged from beneath it, straightened himself up and declared the play 'done' as the pages fell from his hands and landed on the floor like an open fan.

'Come on, let's all go out, let's celebrate,' he said. Arms linked, the five of us made our way down the suburban high street and into the local fish and chip shop. Instead of the usual newspaper wrapping and staining our food with the print, we sat at a Formica table, ate off lightweight white china plates using lightweight knives and forks, and it was one of the happiest hours of my life.

The first night arrived and you could have cut the tension with a knife. I sat on the bottom step of the staircase with my brothers and watched as our parents left the house. The colourful shirts Dad usually wore were often a tad on the scrunched side, absent-mindedly buttoned through the wrong buttonhole, his baggy corduroys held up by a redundant and lonely tie, pleased at last to be of service; and to save precious time in the morning, his striped pyjamas could be found trailing at the bottom of his trousers. But that night was different. That night he could have given any matinee idol a run for his money. Unrecognisably scrubbed, he wore a dinner jacket that Maeve had had made for him especially for the occasion. She was wearing a new dress and looked as well turned out and glamorous as ever.

I had already seen the play at one of the previews, but hadn't really understood it, although the words sounded familiar, and reminded me of him. We had gone together, Dad and I, and as clichéd as it now sounds, someone stood on the stage before the play began and called out, 'The author is in the audience. Let's ask him to say a few words.' Dad walked up the centre aisle and on to the stage, as I smiled at the elderly couple sitting beside me. 'My daughter is with me tonight,' is all I remember.

As Mervyn and Maeve walked to the station to catch the train 'up to town' our whistles and catcalls followed them into the distance. The night was heavy with significance and we all felt it. Everyone was longing for a success. The first night went well, the audience responded enthusiastically, and the cast, including Colin Gordon, Zena Walker and Kenneth Williams, were sure they had a hit on their hands.

After Maeve's relatives treated them to a celebratory dinner at Prunier's, they arrived home, exhausted by the euphoria of the evening. Early the next morning Maeve went out to buy the papers. Every paper gave an extensive review. This was the man who had written *Titus Groan* and *Gormenghast*, the illustrator described by many as the greatest living. Sadly, they ranged from lukewarm to sneeringly unimpressed. The dismissal was final and, as my mother read out the words of the judicious, something snapped.

My father crumbled, metaphorically and physically. In spite of his astonishingly modest view of himself, and the fact that he had taken previous criticisms with a healthy dose of salt and good humour (although my mother didn't, and found it impossible to be objective, sanguine or less than murderous when it came to *any* criticism of her husband or children), those opinions mattered. When I woke, a doctor had been called, and this time I watched with horror from the top of the stairs. My mother, her face ashen with fear, was holding my father, attempting to pacify him, as he sat in his leather armchair outside his study and shook uncontrollably. My leaden feet became rooted to the spot as I stared at this terrifyingly naked tableau being played out twenty steps below, and an awful wave of panic washed over me. My brothers and some friends of theirs took me out for the day and we walked in silence. We crossed a bridge that I always visualise as a pretty, arched and slatted Japanese walkway over to safety, but in reality was a nondescript, flat bridge, carrying my silent brothers, their friends and me over to nothing. I looked down at the curling waves that a group of ducklings, hurrying to keep pace with their mother, had made in the water, and envied the simplicity of their journey.

When we got home, Mervyn had been sedated and taken to hospital (a recurring leitmotif throughout my later childhood) and diagnosed with a complete breakdown. For the next twelve years, with intermittent visits home, he languished in dozens of hospitals, the husband and father we knew gone like a puff of smoke, to be replaced by someone who had partly retreated into another world, somewhere we couldn't join him.

It is hard, and I am trying, not to romanticise a father who was larger than life, a buccaneer with a heart and soul bursting through his chest like a tornado – not the perfect father for a girl who liked life to be comfortable, but the perfect father for a girl who lived and breathed for love and laughter. He had managed effortlessly to make sure his daughter felt adored and appreciated, pretty and funny. By seven I felt all these things, even if they were all to be lost one morning in the blink of an eye. These feelings had maturated and he had done his job.

A different life began, and so we adjusted. I carried on with my childhood, my brothers with their teenage life, and our mother with the nightmare she was enduring. She was thirty-nine years old and, with hindsight, I wonder how she managed to make it all seem so easy. But her magnanimous approach to life made it impossible for her to view herself as a hard-done-by woman. Her sense of humour was too finely tuned, her temperament too philosophical. Her sadnesses were not indulged or interpreted; there was no time for that. She just faced things full on and got on with it. But she missed my father desperately. Her days were fitted around hospital visits. 'Do I look all right?' she'd ask me, taking as much care with her appearance as if this were a first date. She took a wicker basket filled with chocolates and fruit, and a book of his poetry, so she could read to him and attempt to jog a memory confused by drugs and illness.

Arriving home, her swollen eyes hidden by sexy dark glasses, her body exhausted from worry and lack of sleep, she'd kick off her shoes and lie down next to me. With our arms wrapped around each other, hot tears smudging my face, she'd tell me how each visit had gone. Her style and elegance never deserted her and as I lay coiled in her arms, I could smell the Arpège, Miss Dior and Chanel No. 5 that she mixed with alacrity, hating rules of any kind, especially rules that said she shouldn't mix scents or look like a woman enjoying life. Her respect for herself and others remained intact; to let herself go would have spelt defeat, would have marked the beginning of the end.

The diagnosis for Mervyn ranged from senile dementia (he was forty-five) to encephalitis lethargica – sleeping sickness (thought to be contracted during an epidemic sweeping China at the time of Mervyn's childhood, laying dormant for thirty years and precipitated by a shock) – and back to breakdown. Through all of this, she made my life happy, more than happy, wonderful, a life jam-packed with fun and gentle anarchy, in a house where the ambiance she created was warm and exciting, where our friends could come and go, feeling free and important, where the conversations carried on as before, and where her intense love for my father was unwavering. The loneliness, the frustration, the despair, the exhaustion and the longing to be free of the constant supervision and care for her husband must have been present at times, but it appeared to me that however much he fell, dribbled, shook, wept, she never faltered for a single moment in her wholehearted respect and pride for the man she was married to. I couldn't have put it into words or thoughts then; all I knew was that she was the best company on earth, that there was nothing small about her. There was a generosity of spirit, a feeling of naughtiness and a passionate quality that was both romantic and baldly realistic. We began to talk endlessly, and it was the beginning of the conversations that would last our whole lifetime together.

I had my friends, my brothers theirs. Life went on. Dad came home for a while then went to a new hospital – Friern

Barnet, Banstead, Virginia Water, the Maudsley – endless awful places, where corridors went on for miles, where walls were painted a mossy green, a touching attempt at some sort of calm and serenity in the madhouses. I was taken to visit him in these places, where anguished men and women roamed the corridors screaming and laughing, or sat in chairs, sometimes silently, sometimes violently, rocking rhythmically to the beat of some inner torment. One man ran from one end of the corridor to the other in a ceaseless bid for freedom. The smell of desertion and loneliness was awful. Mervyn was permanently terrified and often sedated. He hated and feared the electric shock treatment Maeve had been advised was the right thing for him, and he longed for our visits.

I was confident and optimistic, certain this was all just temporary. All it needed was prayer and patience, and he would be well again. The thought that he might never recover too horrible to contemplate.

Dear darling,

I have been ½ drugged since I last wrote to you so I haven't much to report. I have had 9 injections and feel like a pin-cushion. Today is lovely outside. Wish I were out in it. Had to see the 'Dr' today and had a lot of Tests. 'Say 7345-2176 backwards', 'Put in your own words', 'People who live in glass houses shouldn't throw stones' etc., all of which I passed.

I miss you all very much.

The ward nurses (all men) have pet phrases which they keep on repeating 'I'm out for blood' (injections etc).

It looks as though I've got to the end of stage 1 – the

rest period and treatment. The Dr is OK but not very sympathique. But all will be well.

Letters are allowed here – in fact it's very lax. I love your notes and the love you envelop me in. My thoughts are all for you, I adore and love you.

Please give my love to the boys (and the girl) I love them all. A Chinese man has just come on to our ward, maybe he speaks Mandarin. God bless you. All will come right and we will storm the citadels together.

This is going to be a great spring in our lives.

Mervyn

More letters came, almost daily.

Maeve, more than ever before I want you now. It is beyond all falling in love. It is a yearning such as I have never known before. I have almost lost my identity. I long for your white arms around my neck. The male nurses are pleasant but I am afraid of something subtler – it is the smell of the place – its miles and miles of corridors – the expression on the faces some of whom have been here for years.

I will never write about mad people again. I am in a kind of dream or nightmare and I yearn for your touch.

Maeve, never! Never again! It has done something to me, or rather it has frightened me a bit to be under the same roof with those in other wards – perhaps it's because I have played too much round the edge of madness. O I could cry to be free. I have had 4 electric treatments. I don't like them much – but I believe they do good. O days! DAYS! Roll along.

86

Tell the children I loved their letters. I long for my family again.

God bless you

God bless all of you

From your own husband

Mervyn.

Paloma Picasso

Elena was my best friend and, from the age of three until she ran away to Gretna Green to marry, we were inseparable. Without a trace of awkwardness in situations that would have frightened other children of our age, she helped me with my father. She tied his shoelaces, helped him on and off chairs, wiped his face, but, more importantly, she understood. She became a part of our family, as a few years later I became a part of hers. Summer days were spent in my garden enacting scenes from *South Pacific*. The sissy 'Some Enchanted Evening' and 'Younger than Springtime' were sung solo with a slightly bored 'get on with it' undertone, and the more stirring 'There is Nothing Like a Dame', 'Happy Talk' and 'I'm Gonna Wash That Man Right Out of my Hair' were sung in duet with genuine gusto. Dances were choreographed and costumes assembled as we rehearsed our roles over and over again until the sun went down. Winter nights were spent in the attic, where the dressing-up box was kept. The painted trunk was heaving with glamour – the jet beads, fake pearls, stilettos, Chinese dresses, bras, petticoats, evening gowns, trilby hats, riding boots, army jackets, parasols and suspender belts dressed

Elena and me in our make-believe world for years to come.

We were both passionate readers and would sit for hours discussing plots and characters, then pull costumes from the trunk and act out scenes from our meticulously chosen passages. There wasn't much variation in our choice of book, so the wonderful *Flowers for Mrs Harris*, *The Woodbegoods*, *The Treasure Seekers*, *Five Children and It*, *Black Beauty*, *Little Women*, *The Secret Garden* and *What Katy Did* became a staple enough diet for a thousand wintry nights, and for me a necessary escape from the reality downstairs.

I attended St Elphege's, a small Catholic prep school and, being reared on miracles, I mentioned Lourdes to my mother as a possible answer to Dad's illness. She seemed disinterested. It was all so clear to me. If the doctors were finding everything such a mystery, if they couldn't make him better, surely a pilgrimage was the answer. If not Lourdes, then I would have to find the solution for myself. I trod barefoot through a nettle patch, I drank curdled milk and I stood in an empty church with my arms outstretched, begging Our Lady to speak to her son on my behalf. I watched Dad for signs of returning health, but nothing changed. His on-the-spot shuffling only became worse, and it was impossible to believe I hadn't been heard or, worse, I had been heard but I'd been ignored. I felt insignificant, wounded, embarrassed. I saw myself as an irrelevance, a child not worth wasting a miracle on. All of a sudden I began to lose hope, knowing that nothing would ever be the same again.

We didn't move about, change schools or friends; everything remained constant. It was only Dad who changed. Life was structured, there were parameters, I could rely on the things I'd always relied on, and those things became more important as he became more fragile – jacks on a Friday night after Brownies, the extra half hour I was allowed to stay up to watch *Take Your Pick*, and, if he was at home, learning to ignore Dad's look of abject depression as I sat screaming at the television, 'Open the box! Open the box!'

We used our garden like I've never used a garden before or since. Summer and winter we were out there, Sebastian and Fabian on stilts, chasing after me on my three-wheeled bicycle, scaring me with their huge, loping footsteps, until they caught up. Days were spent searching for 'Torty' our beloved tortoise, eventually finding him hidden in the dense jungle that was the end of our garden. I would carry him back to the smart end, with his feet wriggling and his head dancing back and forth like a metronome fixed on 'grave'. He sat on my lap good-naturedly, his adorable, prehistoric face resigned to another bout of kissing, as I struggled to feed him lettuce and dress his extendable neck in a polka-dot bandana. His soulful eyes glanced longingly at the stretch ahead of him and the slow walk back to his hiding place. Finally, I would release him, and begin to worry all over again about our next meeting and when it might be. He must have become fed up with me because one day he disappeared altogether and, after weeks of frantic searching, I had to face the awful truth: that he'd left home for a place more suited to his temperament. I still miss him.

Dad had made us all a car at various stages of our lives and mine had been carved from the end of a tree trunk. I remember how, when well, he'd dug furiously with a knife and hammer until the innards were removed, and then sanded the interior and flattened the seat until it was smooth enough for me to sit on to drive. I had a tricycle wheel for steering, and pedals made from halved peach cans. I had running-boards and an indicator and I drove all over the world in that elegant shooting-brake, planted under the chestnut tree.

There was an air-raid shelter at the bottom of the garden that Sebastian and Fabian had turned into a nightclub. Digging had gone on for months and when it was finally completed, I discovered it was to be a members-only club. Female and pretty seemed to be the only criteria, but membership was very definitely not open to me, so I sat cross-legged on the lawn making daisy-chains and watching the never-ending stream of giggling girls making their way down to this underground hotspot. In the sitting room I was made to sit on an upright chair facing the television, and ordered not to turn around or look at my brothers and their girlfriends sitting behind me on the sofa. The unlit room was silent, apart from the sporadic giggles coming from the sofa and, intrigued, I sometimes broke the rules to sneak a quick peep at the tedious fumbling that went on interminably.

Sebastian and Fabian were teddy boys, with three-quarter length jackets, quiffs and suede shoes. Sebastian called himself John, Fabian called himself Mungo and I was Roxanne. Embarrassed as she was, my mother tried to remember to call us by our new names. The boys were lean and handsome, and my popularity soared when girls of fifteen and sixteen, who under any other circumstances would never have given me a second thought, discovered I was their sister. They smoked and drank and listened to Bill Hailey and Buddy Holly, the Everly Brothers and Duane Eddy, and they taught me how to jive. Since I was so much lighter than any of their girlfriends, I sailed through their legs and spun under their arms in an arabesque of perfect rhythm. If we were alone, and 'Slave-time' was over for the day, I loved nothing better than sitting on the sofa, sandwiched between them, watching *I Love Lucy* and *Bilko* and, if I promised not to tell Mum, they allowed me to stay up for *Dragnet*. 'Slave-time' was the centuries-old pastime familiar to any youngest child, a game you felt flattered to be a part of. You felt proud when the timed sprint up and down the stairs to collect forgotten items from your sibling's bedroom was faster than the day before – when running baths of the right temperature, answering the telephone, lighting a cigarette, lying to girlfriends and making sandwiches might have given a clue that 'slave-time' wasn't a game that benefited you at all.

I was as close to Sebastian and Fabian as I was able to be, considering the age difference. I hero-worshipped them. What they thought of me is harder to say. They were just thrilling presences that flitted in and out of my life with an avuncular concern for my well-being. They were very different characters – Sebastian, funny, quick-talking and impatient like Maeve; Fabian, funny, slow-talking and patient like Mervyn. Fabian was particularly kind, allowing me to think he couldn't think of anything he'd rather be doing than spending time with his little sister. Sebastian found it more difficult. I was an irritant, a small child, almost ten years his junior, who got in the way and always needed looking after. All that changed when I reached sixteen. All of a sudden it was as if he'd woken from a dream, and I became someone vaguely interesting, someone who, despite his earlier boredom, he began rather to enjoy.

Dad came home off and on, but I don't remember when or for how long. Things he said are clearer. 'Make it sexy, darling,' he would say to Maeve, shorthand for three or four scoops of Horlicks in his bedtime drink. His tooth was exceptionally sweet, although he was never anything but thin. Food didn't interest him much, a trait perhaps left over from the constant interruptions for meals that kept him from his drawing as a boy. What he liked was dripping spread on to a chunk of bread, cheese sandwiches, egg and bacon, anything that was quick and uncomplicated, so that eating was out of the way and he could get on with the things that did interest him. Unkindly, we all took advantage of this and he probably died thinking the only chocolates manufactured were lime cordial, strawberry cup and orange cream, since by the time it was his turn to choose, everything else had gone. He was a man of simple tastes, and everything that excited him happened internally. On the subjects he loved – poetry, painting, trees, birds and people – he was enormously knowledgeable. Before he became ill, every walk was strewn with observations on the trees we passed or the birds we heard, all instantly recognisable to him. 'Look at that elm, that maple, that beech, that ash, that cedar, that oak, Clare . . . notice how the leaves have ziggy-zaggy edges and the bark looks like an elephant's skin. Imagine how long that old boy has stood there, imagine what he knows . . . Ssh! Listen, can you hear the song thrush? Listen darling, do you hear it? It's singing just for us.'

Dad coming back and forth from hospital became so familiar it was almost as if he was in the navy. It was an inextricable part of our lives. The ambulances came and went, and we all seemed to be either laughing or crying; there didn't seem to be much in between. In hospital, art therapy classes must have been torture for Mervyn. It wasn't anyone's fault, but being taught how to hold a pencil properly, and unable to protest, must have been for him the very nadir of ignomony.

When he was home, television, ironically, became a comfort and release for him. He would sit watching *Steptoe and Son*, *Hancock's Half Hour* and his particular favourite Stanley Unwin, and I would hear him laughing out loud as he had in earlier times when watching his heroes the Marx Brothers, whom he talked about, and quoted, for my entire childhood.

Day-to-day life carried on as usual, family jokes remained intact. Maeve still woke me in the morning with a row of Sugar Puffs where her teeth should be, her pretty face distorted by a mass of rotting gnashers, her cackling witch's laugh filling the room before she finally dissolved in giggles at her own funniness. She still warned me that naughtiness or interrupting adults' conversation would result in her picking me up from school wearing one of those concertina rain-hats found in crackers, the ones old ladies wear, tied tight under her chin, even in the summer, even without rain. And Dad, if he was at home, still attempted the same old jokes at mealtimes. 'See that man over there eating spaghetti? No? Well, you see the spaghetti.' And, 'Waiter, waiter, there's a fly in my soup. Please remove the soup.' Wonderfully feeble, and wonderfully familiar, all Marx Brothers, and probably all misquoted.

I was eight when I had my first real taste of adventure. Allowed to do some simple shopping for Maeve on Saturday mornings, I walked down the drive, turned right out of the gates and looked for a woman to cross me over the road, and another (after I'd done my shopping) to cross me back. I had to hold her hand and I had to remember my pleases and thank-yous. These were the conditions. All this was relatively easy. It was only when I opened the brown-inked scrap of paper that my problems began.

10 oz soiled bweets
1 jot of pam
10 bashers of racon
20 Moo Daurier and a mox of batches
1 lb un-balted sutter
The *Nimes* tewspaper and a punch of fretty plowers

I queued in grocers, bakers and newsagents attempting to decipher Maeve's lists while shopkeepers looked at me pityingly and I leapt to her defence. I understood the joke even if they didn't. The list was always different, half the things she didn't even need, but my English improved and I was free.

I never played with toys or dolls – I didn't like them, I only liked books and dressing up – so I was astonished by my reaction when I spotted a doll in Harrod's toy department who weaved an instantaneous spell over me. I named her Paloma, after Paloma Picasso, who had been born in the same year as I was. I had once overheard my mother discussing the beauty of her name, and was very irritated by the bluntness of my name in comparison. Clare Peake – it sounded so stark, like a judge hitting his gavel, such an angry name. When I complained to my mother, she nodded her head from side to side, 'Ah! That's where you're wrong – what it is, is a powerful name, a name potent in its very starkness.' I neither understood nor agreed.

Paloma stood in her red satin box, distant and self-contained, as though thinking: 'I've got all the time in the world. I'll leave my box when the right girl comes along.'

95

Maeve must have noticed because when my birthday came around in May the usual treasure hunt for my presents led me to Paloma. I had searched under cushions, in airing cupboards, in tea caddies and under beds. Cryptic clues, written on small scraps of paper, finally led me to the attic. I reached into the dressing-up box and underneath the clothes I felt a large oblong parcel. I had never seen a mesmeric doll before seeing her; there was something in her dark, soulful eyes that gave her the power to come alive. She was dressed in a crimson velvet, box-pleated skirt on top of a stiff white net petticoat, a yellow-and-white gingham shirt, white ankle socks edged with a frill, and black patent leather shoes. She had brown freckles on her pale, matt skin and her knees and elbows were dimpled. As I brushed her lustrous black hair, she listened to the worries I felt powerless to do anything about, and her silent wisdom soothed me in my moments of anxiety. Paloma fell from the attic window one afternoon and broke into a thousand pieces, her legs and arms torn from their sockets, her china face smashed to bits. She was dispatched to the dolls' hospital but, when she arrived home, she looked too sad and too patched and I couldn't face her any more.

Childhood was awash with the constant trickling of adult problems. Words hovered in the atmosphere. They meant nothing to me but had seeped into the subconscious: myxomatosis, Papa Doc and the Mau Mau, the Suez crisis, Hungary, the Kinsey Report. When Maeve wasn't painting, she was packing up parcels or giving blood. Fold-up tables were erected in the garden and covered in odds and ends to sell for Hungarians whom she told me had lost their homes. A steady stream of buyers queued for this variation on a boot sale. The money was added to the spare change already saved in jam jars. As each jar filled, the money, collected in little hessian tie-up bags, was taken to a crisis centre, along with the jumpers, hats, scarves and socks she'd knitted for refugee children. What they made of these elaborately designed donations is hard to imagine. The ashen face resulting from her blood-letting sessions continued until a year or so before she died. 'My blood type, AB negative, is rather rare you see, darling – well naturally it is! No ordinary blood for ME thanks,' she laughed as she made her way to the hospital.

Meanwhile, Sebastian, aged twenty, was to become a father. Carin, a German au pair girl, had discovered her pregnancy after Sebastian had gone to live in Sweden to learn the language. It had never been a serious romance, and she had found herself thrown out of the house she was living in, the scandalised family knocking on our door one tea-time to inform Maeve of the outrage inflicted on their household. As I cycled round and round the garden, I saw their flushed and furious faces through the French windows. Their mouths spewed angry words, and their offended eyes bore down on Maeve as she held her head in her hands. I couldn't imagine what these dreary-looking strangers were doing in our house, and what they were saying to my silent mother that had upset her so.

Sebastian returned from Sweden and Carin packed her bags and came to live with us. She arrived as a virtual stranger but, over the months, we all grew to love her. She had had a very sad beginning. When she was four, her mother had been killed in front of her when a tank full of Russian soldiers entering Berlin had mowed her down, and although at the time I knew nothing of the tragedy of her early life, it clung to her in all kinds of ways.

She had a proud, gentle nature and a melancholy that made her seem older than her nineteen years. Although beautiful and majestic, she was completely unaware of it. Her father, when learning of her pregnancy, wanted nothing more to do with her, so effectively parentless, my mother did her very best to make Carin feel wanted and cared for during this lonely time.

I was ignorant of the rigmaroles of pregnancy and birth, and watched in confusion as her stomach grew bigger. There were attempts at explanation but I wasn't ready to understand and, without any idea of what was going on, Carin and I became friends. Near her due date, she travelled home to Berlin where Vincent was born, but every year Carin and Vincent came to England to stay with us, or Maeve went to Berlin to visit them, doing everything, emotionally and financially, for her first grandchild and his beloved mother that she possibly could.

One morning a few years later, a black-edged envelope was delivered to the house and, as she read the letter, I saw Maeve's face drain of colour. Tears poured down her cheeks as she told me that Carin had died after a botched operation. She was twenty-six and Vincent, now motherless like Carin, was seven. Maeve wanted him to live with us but the German authorities wouldn't allow it. Sebastian was not yet married or settled and, because of Mervyn's illness, our home was considered an unsuitable place to bring up a child. Although Sebastian and Carin had previously discussed marriage, both felt it wasn't the right thing for either of them, so when Carin died, the authorities were free to decide Vincent's fate. An elderly, childless German couple adopted Vincent, with the proviso that there was to be no more contact. My parents never saw him again. After Maeve died, her will requested that her and Mervyn's first grandchild be traced, and so began a close relationship between Sebastian and his son that continues to this day.

Pocket money was a regular and unchanging amount. The sixpence I was given on a Friday afternoon had to last all week, but with that respectable amount I was able to buy as many sweets as I wanted. Naturally, they were all eaten by four-fifteen the same day, but Maeve was strict on this, and didn't give in to demands for weekday sweets, thinking perhaps that by the following Friday my teeth would have recovered from the bombardment.

Unfortunately, when I saw something I wanted to save up for, sweets had to be forgotten. I had spotted a brooch in Woolworth's that would set me back an exorbitant nineteen shillings and sixpence. It was exquisite and dramatic and worth every penny, and I wanted to buy it for Maeve's fortieth birthday. Assembled together and pasted into one giant flower were diamonds, rubies, emeralds, sapphires and pearls. The assistant in Woolworth's agreed with me that it was priceless, and put it under the counter, promising to hold on to it until I had all the money. I couldn't accumulate that amount of cash by pocket money alone, so I saved it through a variety of 'get rich quick' schemes. I made scent by stamping on flower petals with my bare feet, and sold the eighth of an inch of grey sludge in jam jars to my parents' friends. I gave impromptu but well-rehearsed renditions of 'Fever' with enormous empathy for Peggy Lee's every nuance. I sat on a stool outside the house and sold vanilla and strawberry cornets to passers-by, until eventually I had saved it all. Maeve looked staggered as she opened the large cardboard box, but I couldn't read her face – her expression was unfamiliar. In the blink of an eye, there it was, a look I recognised, as she declared it the most beautiful thing she had ever laid eyes on. From that day forward, it was pinned on to everything she wore, and I remember the feeling, as a child, that I had an eye, that somehow I had managed to find a thing of such extraordinary taste and discrimination that my heart swelled with pride. Years later, I remembered the brooch, the enormity and hideousness of the thing, and asked her what she had done about it all those years before. Sometimes she kept it on, she said; who cared what people thought? Sometimes she wasn't brave enough, and hid it in her bag as she left the house. The pity on strangers' faces quickly reminded her which option she'd chosen.

On one of those nights, in the midst of the Profumo scandal, she was invited to a dinner party where Mandy Rice-Davies was one of the guests. I'd heard the name bandied about for months. She, Christine Keeler, John Profumo, Stephen Ward and a Russian man whose name I could never remember, were the only subject people ever seemed to talk about. Maeve described Mandy Rice-Davies as very amusing company and extremely attractive in the flesh, adding that as they were talking, out of the corner of her eye, she looked down and with horror realised she had forgotten to remove the brooch.

With my new-found sense of the aesthetic, the plastic trophies engraved to 'The best Mum in the world' and 'The best Dad in the world' sat proudly alongside the Chinese dragons and ancient brass bowls in our sitting room, with as much right to their position as anything else. Over the years, whenever they were given anything dreadful, they found it easier to keep it, use it, display it, and, in the end, become fond of it. That way we had things that seemed perfectly natural to us because we were used to them, but must have seemed extraordinary to visitors. A knitted shepherdess with a two-inch staff covered our lavatory rolls, and there were other *objets d'art* and frilly knick-knacks that Mr Forbes, my mother's octogenarian cleaner, had given her that she didn't have the heart to throw away. They just lived and what came their way fitted in. People's feelings were so much more important than taste.

On visits home from whichever hospital he happened to be living in at the time, Dad would occasionally accompany me to Mass, but as the non-Catholic in the family he found it hard to understand the rules. His own upbringing in the Congregationalist Church had been rather forgotten, and overpowered by the powerfully insistent Catholicism all around him. There was so much bobbing up and down going on, he couldn't help but get it wrong. He thought the hymns stodgy and tuneless compared with the more expressive Protestant hymns that he knew, and he found the lack of forgiveness in most of the Catholics he came across pretty terrifying. I became annoyed by his valiant attempts to sing along, always getting the words wrong, and standing as everyone sat, or vice versa. 'Sorry, darling, I thought this was the sitting time. I'll get it right next time,' he whispered, as he stood erect, and the congregation knelt.

But being alone with him was still the best thing on earth. It didn't seem to matter how unsteady he might be, how difficult it was to understand every word he said because, well or unwell, everything was enhanced by his presence. A stroll along the street could unearth fifteen major observations along the way – the formation of the clouds and who they reminded us of; the grey pavement, and how much more satisfying it would be to tread had it been allowed a spot of crimson every ten feet; the melancholia of the worn-out dog, looking the spit of his mistress; the wonderful spire on the otherwise ordinary church; the gleam of a woman's black hair as she glided past. Everything made sense when he was around, and even though I felt in control, the knowledge bleeding from behind his sunken eyes let me know just how wrong I was.

An anonymous gift of money (never proven, but thought to have been sent by Lady Moray) had arrived in the post with a typed proviso that some of it was to be spent on a much-needed holiday for Mervyn and Maeve. They went to Madrid for three weeks, which, to me, felt like a lifetime. I stayed with a friend from school, in a house that was haunted by the mother of a child who had died there years before. She appeared at the foot of my friend's mother's bed every time she gave birth to one of her four babies, and presented herself to the family's youngest child, Clare, as an apparition. We watched from an upstairs window as Clare chatted animatedly in the garden to an unseen but meticulously described woman. A priest exorcised the house some time later but, when I was staying in this ordinary, suburban house, the sensation of being watched and the freezing chill in one particular room was real and very frightening.

Madrid was a great success. The Prado was closed for redecoration, but Walter Starkie gave Mervyn and Maeve an introduction to the curator and they spent an unforgettable day in the deserted gallery being shown around by an elderly attendant. They were introduced to Lady

Lindsay Hogg. Mervyn, unable to resist a beautiful woman, drew several pictures of her, which he then gave her. They arrived home laden with gifts for us. My first Holy Communion was imminent and I was counting the days until I could be 'married to God'. I was given a white wedding dress, a flowered headband, a tiny bag made of beaded flowers, and an embroidered mantilla. 'You know St Theresa,' my father said. 'Umm,' I sanctimoniously replied. 'Well, I saw her thumb pickled in a jar.' But, however thrilled I was with my first Holy Communion dress and all the accessories, they came a close second to the polka-dot flamenco dress, high-heeled shoes and castanets also brought home for me. The break had benefited everyone.

Esperanto Classes

It wasn't just what was happening at home that unsettled me. There were also the fears that kept all children with an active imagination awake in the night, different from the fears children have now, but just as real. When I was growing up, it was polio and the iron lung, a contraption so awful to contemplate it was better not to. Sometimes in the middle of the night I lay awake, restlessly imagining myself being read to in the wee small hours by matron, unable to stop her, my young life ebbing oh so slowly away to the droning on. The books changed through the interminable years from *Black Beauty* to Gibbons' *Decline and Fall*, the mirror that reflected my laboured breathing misting up with fear and claustrophobia. 'You'll end up in an iron lung,' was the playground wisdom for any infraction of the germ rules.

Germs were discussed with enormous reverence in those days, a word not used much around our house, where fussiness was so little in evidence that it left me with a loathing for ridiculously precious behaviour concerning one's health. I couldn't bear being wrapped up or coddled, fretted or fussed over, and, aside from the inevitable childhood diseases, I didn't get stomach aches, 'chills', coughs or colds. All around me people were warning of the dangers lurking on every plate, in every cupboard, in every kiss, but it always seemed to me that the people who gave germs the respect they so clearly deserved were the very same ones rushing off to the doctor's with endless complaints. Our family doctor was of the same opinion. 'What do you do when you drop a sweet on the floor?' he asked me one day. 'You pick it up and eat it, that's what you do,' he answered himself vehemently. 'Too much pernicketiness is going to make us all ill.'

When we ceased tormenting ourselves with thoughts of life in an iron lung, it was being white-slave trafficked to the Belgian Congo. We peered at the location in an atlas, sure in the knowledge that if it were our misfortune to be kidnapped by a raincoated man with a pencil moustache, he would surely be the procurer whose job it was to find small English girls. We would be transported to Africa, where we would end our days being forced to do things rumoured to be too dreadful to describe. I knew a thing or two about peculiar men, having been flashed at once in a nearby park. It had been a nasty shock to be confronted by a dangling chipolata hanging so ostentatiously outside this man's trousers, but almost worse was his stillness, and the glassy look in his eye. Then, as though rehearsed in minute detail from a book of clichés, he covered himself up with the too-large raincoat and ran away, his silly long legs carrying him off to his wife and children, or his invalid mother, as, with a panicky horror, I shrieked with laughter.

Collecting me from school one afternoon, I saw at once that Maeve had been crying. 'Chloe's dead,' she said. She looked utterly defeated. Chloe had been a part of our lives for so long, it was hard to contemplate life without her. She had adapted gamely to every kind of accommodation, every type of geology, from flats to houses, islands to cities, gardens to litter trays and, aged nineteen, she had finally gone. Searching for Mum later in the evening, I found her curled up on the bed of a room I never went into, a box room, a chilly, lifeless room. 'Chloe knew all my secrets,' she said, as the tears spilled from her eyes. 'She was my friend.' I had never seen my mother so heartbroken; it was as if all the sadness over Dad's absence had been softened by Chloe's simple affection and uncomplicated sweetness. She could now cry all the tears she'd held in for so long without reservation.

After a while Katy replaced Chloe, but it wasn't a success, because it never is. It was the first and last real failure we ever had with a cat. Apart from being unaffectionate, she had an unappealing streak of hauteur about her that should have made her interesting, but didn't because she was so immensely dull. Dad said Katy reminded him of Brown Owl, a woman he detested because she'd been angry with me for forgetting my Brownie promise, and had stormed round to the house to complain about this trifling incident. A memory of my father before things changed out of all recognition was his reaction to her. He had been extremely offhand, something I had never seen before, and despite my entreaties, he refused to apologise, saying that any grown woman calling herself Brown Owl without a trace of irony didn't deserve to be apologised to, and Katy, he thought, had the same quality. She was a hygiene officer masquerading as a cat and, although we felt bitterly cruel, it was hard not to feel depressed by her presence. It was mutual. She didn't like us either, and when a couple from the country came to visit, they looked at Katy and Katy looked at them, and a thankful recognition had her diving into their arms, begging them to take her home. Dinah Shore followed soon after, and all was well once again.

Maeve was still regularly going 'up to town', to see friends, go to the cinema or have her weekly Esperanto lesson. It occurs to me now that she was probably one of the three people in the world learning Esperanto but, being an optimist and good at languages, I think she was hoping this universal language would catch on. In the morning, as we walked to school, she practised her Esperanto on me. I spoke in English and she replied in Esperanto and then she would switch to English and describe the film she had seen the night before. Going back and forth, making sure I had the locations and characters accurately, I listened to the story. Some were more difficult to describe than others, especially European films that relied heavily on the mood, but I still have films in my head that I have never seen, and one in particular, *Crin-Blanc*, a film about white horses in the Camargue, I have even dreamed about. Her descriptions were lyrical and thorough and, by the time the credits rolled, I could have given a seminar on the subject.

Dad could sometimes manage the cinema, but it had to be an early showing with fewer people to disturb if he became restless. The theatre was far more complicated, and we almost never risked it. But I was desperate to see *Oliver!* and in 1960 my mother bought three tickets for the opening week. She naively imagined that Dad might be less conspicuous if we were in a box, and if he couldn't settle, at least he wouldn't be disturbing anyone else. I knew every word of every song by heart as the producers had cleverly released the record before the musical had opened. Dad couldn't sit

107

still, and shuffled in and out of the box every few minutes. Mum and I were acutely aware of how off-putting it must have been for the actors, and knew at once we had made a terrible mistake. We were torn between leaving the theatre before the musical got going, ruining something I had been looking forward to for months, or upsetting the cast. At last, thank God, it ended, and as the actors took their curtain calls, Georgia Brown looked up at our box and blew Dad a kiss. There was no mistake and no ridicule. It was aimed right at him, as though somehow she understood. Small kindnesses made life worth fighting for. Maeve couldn't and didn't forget a couple of writers who turned their back on Mervyn as he tried to say hello at parties or literary events. 'He's drunk,' they muttered under their breath or, worse, they could tell he was desperately ill but were too embarrassed or too insensitive to remember their manners. I know my mother found it unbearable to watch her husband cold-shouldered by these ghastly people, and it breaks my heart just to think of it. I had been around this mindless cruelty myself, but when offered by people proud of their brains it was harder to understand. Painters, curiously, never did this, and many heads of art schools tried desperately to keep teaching posts open for him when everyone knew what an impossible situation it was.

Dad and I had always gone to Box Hill together, and occasionally still did. Given the fare and a packed lunch, we'd set off on our journey. Arriving at the pretty station, decorated with colourful flower boxes and looking like something from an H. E. Bates novel, we'd make our way to the hills. It took time as Dad walked so slowly. His on-the-spot shuffling had him stopping every few paces, his legs having gone into spasm. It was also extremely difficult to understand what he was saying and, to avoid the frustration on both sides, we found it easier to recite poetry than have a conversation. Holding hands we ploughed our way up the hills reciting Walter de la Mare's 'The Listeners'. However bright the sunlight, those first few lines never failed to give me shivers that ran right through me.

Is there anybody there? said the Traveller,
Knocking on the moonlit door;
And his horse in the silence champed the grasses
Of the forest's ferny floor:
And a bird flew up out of the turret,
Above the Traveller's head:
And he smote upon the door again a second time;
Is there anybody there? he said.

The same mysterious and oddly comforting feeling applied to one of the other poems that we recited more than any others, Kipling's 'The Way Through the Woods':

They shut the road through the woods
Seventy years ago.
Weather and rain have undone it again,
And now you would never know
There was once a road through the woods
Before they planted the trees.
It is underneath the coppice and heath
And the thin anemones.
Only the keeper sees
That, where the ring-dove broods,
And the badgers roll at ease,
There was once a road through the woods.

Remembering the lines brings everything flooding back. I knew those woods intimately, I had heard that poem over and over again and, as my father's small voice rummaged for the words lodged somewhere in the back of his brain, they eventually tumbled out as they always did, because poetry was salvation for him and never let him down. His depth of knowledge was vast. You only had to open a collection of poetry at random, give him the first line, and he would finish the poem off word for word. He spoke poetry as it should be spoken – not with elaborate flourishes, but with the understanding of a poet, strong, straight, and in control – and he taught me how to speak it. 'Not sing-song, darling,' he said. 'Never sing-song.'

One awful, unforgettable day when I was nine, after nervously guiding Dad up the steps and on to the train on our way to Box Hill, three boys of fourteen or fifteen sat opposite us and sniggered at him throughout the journey. They flicked tiny pieces of paper at him and mimicked his shaking. I didn't know what to do. I wasn't sure if Dad knew what was happening and, if he did, we both pretended not to notice. I managed to hold in the tears flooding my eyes, terrified that he would understand, praying for them to get off the train before us. They did, but my heart was already broken and the feeling of utter bewilderment at how anyone could sink so low was overwhelming.

Mervyn had once written, 'There is a kind of laughter that sickens the soul. Laughter when it is out of control, when it screams and stamps its feet, and sets the bells jangling in the next town. Laughter in all its ignorance and cruelty. Laughter with the seed of Satan in it. It tramples upon shrines; the belly-roarer, it roars, it yells, it is delirious; and yet it is as cold as ice. It has no humour, it is naked noise and naked malice.'

This sort of obscene cruelty was rare, though, and people were mostly very understanding. A few years later, a boy asked me out. He came to the house to collect me and was sitting down when Dad shuffled into the room. He stood up immediately, shook my father's hand and smiled broadly. 'How do you do, sir,' he said. I can't remember who he was, but I will never forget his sensitivity in concealing his shock when a man looking over ninety was introduced as my father.

Drayton Gardens Dreaming

When I was ten my mother decided to move back to central London. Maeve's middle brother, a farmer and property developer, had made an offer for our house so good (£8,000) that it would allow her to buy a house in Chelsea outright. So, with a gigantic spring in her step, she went house-hunting for somewhere she and my father could live forever. The second house she saw was perfect. Number 1, Drayton Gardens. It had a lucky ring to it, a bay tree in the front, a walnut tree in the back, Old Brompton Road at one end, Fulham Road at the other. What more could you possibly want? My mother's excitement was palpable. At last, she was going home. Dad was coming back and forth from hospital regularly now, the final diagnosis being Parkinson's disease. Maeve wanted to be closer to friends whom she could see whenever she wanted, and she felt the need to escape the constraints of suburbia. Sebastian was living in Sweden, Fabian had just begun at Chelsea Art School, and I was the only fly in the ointment. I didn't want to leave my friends behind and I expected to be murdered. London would be cold and unfriendly; it would be full of dangerous men and swarming crowds. Maeve did her best

112

to reassure me. Life would be stimulating; it was a different way of living, but a better way after the claustrophobia of the suburbs.

In fact, some sort of community life was going on behind the apparent anonymity of central London. There was Bobby's corner shop and local restaurants where we were greeted warmly on introducing ourselves as new residents. But on moving day, 25 May 1960, by a stroke of serendipity my eleventh birthday, I was apprehensive and sad. Hating change, I was surprised to find it took less than a month for me to fall hopelessly in love with the house and the area. I went exploring every day and London wooed and flattered me until I was enticed by everything I saw and utterly smitten. I felt as if I were on holiday, everything had that exciting confidence about it, there was something big, generous and alive about it all, and I was on fire with excitement. My mother looked happier than I'd seen her for a long time, and life became easier.

Everywhere was within walking distance. Maeve drew me a map so I could walk to the swimming pool in Manresa Road, where we'd all once lived, and every few days I would go to the tiny library on Old Brompton Road to renew my books. I could walk to the Victoria and Albert Museum, the Natural History and Science Museums and, on Sundays if he were at home, Dad and I would take a stroll to Kensington Gardens to float a paper boat on the round pond or lie back in striped deck chairs listening to the brass band. It wasn't just the cultural cornucopia surrounding me, it was the people, too. The proud old ladies with crimson lipstick painted hard on to their bow-shaped lips, the dignified tramps pushing their lives around in battered prams, the sophisticated men and women jumping into red sports cars, the beatniks carrying guitars and wearing duffel coats, the air of confidence everyone had, the feeling we belonged.

Dad came home for short spells and we had to be vigilant. Maeve would leave him four floors up, sound asleep in their bedroom, as she attempted to paint for an uninterrupted half hour in her tiny basement studio. She painted, on huge canvases, small vignettes from family life, my brothers playing in Indian headgear, women sitting facing each other, wool unfurling around one woman's hands as another wound it into a ball, self-portraits and, later, line drawing after line drawing of Mervyn, a haunted figure. Nothing gave her more pleasure than being in her studio and I loved to watch her paint, just like Dad, a cigarette dangling from her lips, her brow furrowed in concentration.

We *were* vigilant, but on one or two occasions Dad still managed to escape. The moment he opened the front door he was lost. There was a major road to navigate, a road he had already forgotten he knew, so he wandered around the area trying to find his bearings, having no idea of who or where he was. We would rush around the house frantically looking for him, but a moment later the doorbell would ring and there would be Daddy holding the hand of our new pub, restaurant or newsagent friend. His face would light up with pure joy at seeing one of us, as though it had been years, recognising something about us that was familiar, the silver identification bracelet, with his name and address inscribed on it like a lost dog's, having led him home. Then back to hospital, locked doors, routine, drugs and safety.

On Sundays, Mum and I would take our pick where we went to Mass. There was the tiny church within a house in Gloucester Road, or we might be in the mood for St Mary Abbott, or it could be the Brompton Oratory, all within walking distance. But midnight Mass was always at the Brompton Oratory, because we had more fun there. The drunks would stumble in through the revolving doors; round and round they went, giggling noisily or whispering loudly, or ordering each other to hush, and then singing at the top of their voices 'Away in a Manger' and 'Silent Night'. After it was over we would wrap ourselves up and stroll to the Rembrandt Hotel for a celebratory drink – a glass of champagne for Maeve, a Babycham for me. Christmas Day by then, we would take a slow walk home. It was always my stocking that I was most excited about. Maeve had been buying odds and ends all year long, filling this magical, misshapen, laddered, thick old woman's stocking with frilly knickers, and scent, and sweet-smelling soap, and bangles from the Indian shop in Bute Street, and lipsticks, and eyeliner, and a compact, and paperback poetry, and lace hankies, and talc with an enormous puff, and tartan tights, and red tights, and striped tights, and paisley tights. It usually lay hidden under towels in the airing cupboard but on Christmas Eve I went to sleep with this horizontal lump lying on my toes, promising me such delights when I woke.

Maeve took me to see her friends close by. Quentin Crisp lived a few minutes away in the famously dusty little room in Beaufort Street that, as far as I can remember, had only a bed, a chair and a typewriter to furnish it. The gas fire would be lit and Quentin would make us tea to accompany the cake Maeve had brought with her, the two of them chatting away like the old friends they were. I found him easy to talk to and conversation flowed. Although he was obviously unconventional to look at, I don't remember being particularly thrown by his clothes or manner, which strikes me as strange now. They first met in Fitzrovia in the thirties, when Mervyn

115

employed him as an artist's model, and later Quentin asked Mervyn to illustrate *All This and Bevin Too*, a satirical pamphlet he had written. Quentin wrote about this in his autobiography, *The Naked Civil Servant*:

> The idea seemed to need something else to make it worth a publisher's while, so I tried to ensnare Mr Peake into illustrating it. He was at that time the most fashionable illustrator in England. In spite of this, he frequently sat at the Bar-B-Q in Chelsea and was not in the least inaccessible. When talking to him, I allowed it to seem that Messrs Ivor Nicholson & Watson had already commissioned the book and he declared himself willing to illustrate anything that was certain of appearing in print. These words had hardly issued from his lips when I leapt up and ran all the way to Manchester Square to tell the publishers that Mr Peake was simply dying to illustrate a book I had written. They expressed their interest in anything that Mr Peake chose to work upon. When the book came out, anxious to know if sales were booming, I crept into Hatchard's where a pile of copies was on display. To my delight there was a man staring at the uppermost of these. This, however, turned out to be Mr Peake.

My mother's best friend, the poet Barbara Norman, was trickier. A great friend of Quentin's, too, I found her slightly frightening. The niece of Sir Montague Norman, Governor of the Bank of England, she was small, dark and fiery, with a smoky laugh, and a gigantic personality. Maeve hinted at severed ties with an aristocratic family, and her abdication from a philistine upbringing that never suited her. My parents were immensely fond of Barbara and considered her poetry to be woefully underrated.

Maeve described meeting Barbara for the first time when they were both seventeen. 'She was living in a terrible room, with everything in a filthy state . . . The first time I met her she took out a piece of jagged glass, and began combing her hair with a comb that only had two teeth left.'

Years later, at my twenty-first birthday party, she arrived, a fragile little bird, dressed in a child's dress and cardigan. With furious jet eyes, she scanned the room, fixed her powerful gaze on the people she didn't recognise and aggressively accused them of 'not knowing Maeve and Mervyn at all' (Mervyn had died two years previously) and demanding an explanation for what they were doing there. I was extremely embarrassed, but there was as much chance of Maeve throwing her out as of her enjoying a darts tournament. Things settled down and the rest of the evening went swimmingly.

One night, when things were going badly for Barbara, she arrived in the middle of the night, rapped at the door and asked for money. Mum handed her whatever she had with no outward sign of annoyance. As I stood at the top of the stairs staring down at our night visitor, my mother closed the door and, noticing my silent and bleary-eyed questioning, answered defensively, precluding any query I might have, with a resounding 'She's my friend.' She was similarly loyal to the little coterie of men she had working for her in one capacity or another, and became livid if the integrity of the literary agent, accountant, upholsterer, builder, picture-framer, gallery owner or restaurateur were questioned by Sebastian, who suspected his mother was 'being done'. Hating a Doubting Thomas disposition and hating meanness

117

even more, she would say to Sebastian, 'I like him, don't be so beastly,' desperately hurt on behalf of yet another person taking her for a ride.

Sebastian was only doing his best to protect his mother from the circling sharks who had cottoned on long ago that when it came to easy prey, Mervyn and Maeve were a dream combination. But where Mervyn's work was concerned, Maeve's sixth sense was extremely accurate. She could become most annoyed when he took yet another picture off the wall and gave it to anyone who expressed a liking for it. She felt sure that certain people took advantage of his generosity and had some foreknowledge of this habit of his. And yet gypsies, door-to-door salesmen and people down on their luck hit gold when Maeve answered the door, as she listened to the stories sympathetically, believed everything they said, then reached for her purse and gave them whatever she had. But the relationship Maeve and Mervyn had with money was always a distrustful one. They needed it but they didn't like it. Returning home from a night out, when finances were tenuous to say the least, I found Maeve standing in Dad's studio, holding a lit match and in the process of burning a five-pound note. 'That's what I think of you – you filthy lucre,' she was saying to herself. 'I hate you bloody stuff. Respect money? What on earth would anyone respect money for?'

In June 1960, a month after we moved to Drayton Gardens, I introduced myself to the manager of the Marengo restaurant across the road. I wanted to take a look at the menu to make sure that the prawn cocktail, scampi and chips, and vanilla ice cream and chocolate sauce would be available if I brought Maeve there for her birthday. Everything was, and so were the sweet peas the manager

118

had thoughtfully placed on the table after asking about her favourite flower. Tying a blindfold round her eyes, I guided Maeve across the Old Brompton Road and into the Marengo. Throughout the meal an exquisite man observed us. It would have been hard not to have noticed the effusion with which Maeve greeted every course, and after we finished our meal this wondrous creature made his way to our table and put his hands on my shoulders. 'I have been watching you,' he said. 'Is this a celebration?' We told him of the occasion and he asked whether he could buy us both a glass of champagne. We chatted for a while, my first taste of champagne going straight to my head and, as he left the restaurant smiling and waving, Maeve looked at me. 'We'll remember today, darling; that was a Russian ballet dancer called Rudolph Nureyev . . . isn't he beautiful?'

Boarding School Blues and Books

Maeve had found schools locally where I could begin in September but I couldn't bear to be parted from my best friend Elena and decided I would rather be a boarder at the school she was going to as a day girl than lose her. I had just failed my 11-plus, which meant fees would have to be paid. If I'd passed, I would have had grammar school status at the same school. In the week she died, Maeve recalled the day we got the results. My friends and I had already decided that, whatever the outcome, we would walk as a group to each of our houses to let our parents know this life-changing news. Sadly, all but one of us had passed and, not wanting to display my disappointment or minimise their success, I trailed behind, trudging from one house to another, humiliated by the sympathetic kindness shown to me by my friends' mothers. Smiling weakly at their daughters' success, I finally collapsed into the last house, my own, waving a feeble goodbye to my friends and sobbing into my mother's outstretched arms, 'I'm not good at anything, am I?' Desperately attempting to conjure up a rapid list of my hidden talents, Maeve reeled them off, adding, 'and you're good at love, darling, and that's the best thing to be good at,'

Maeve and Mervyn – Maida Vale flat, 1938.

Maeve and Mervyn – Berlin Zoo, 1937.

My sweetest, my most dear darling Maeve.

Today you will be going into the Nursing Home. I hope that everything will work smoothly & that everyone will be gentle to you, my dear little wife. I have had no definite news as to whether I can come or not but I will do my utmost. How wonderful it was to be able to talk to you last night, dear Maeve. As I told you, I was speaking from that family I told you about. They gave me high tea when I dropped in about 6pm and I told them about you. I want to tell everyone about you — about your beauty — your sweetness, your paintings.

Are you feeling very imminent, Maeve. Do you feel worried or can you detatch yourself at all. Oh darling, how I love you, How I love you.

Perhaps when this reaches you the little baby will be borne.

Oh Maeve.

You are in my heart, darling.
I am loving you more than I
have ever done before. Bless
you — Oh my sweetheart,
bless you. **Bless** you.

I am longing for your
release. I am longing
for news, & to be with you.
Maeve. I am in
love. Deeply. Un-endingly,
For ever & Ever.
your Mervyn

(above and previous page) Letter from Mervyn to Maeve from
army barracks – Blackpool, January 1940.

(left) Mervyn – Sark, circa 1949.

(below) Mervyn drawing – Trafalgar Studios, Manresa Road, 1946.

Maeve and Mervyn, circa 1950.

Mervyn and Clare, circa 1952.

(above) Clare –
Wallington, 1954.

(right) Maeve and
Clare – Wallington,
1956.

Maeve and Clare,
godmother
Laura's garden,
Buckinghamshire,
1957.

Maeve at Grand Greve – Sark holiday, 1958.

Clare – Sark holiday, 1958.

(above) Fabian,
Maeve and
Sebastian –
Wallington,
1959/1960.

(right) Clare
– polyphoto,
Harrods, 1960.

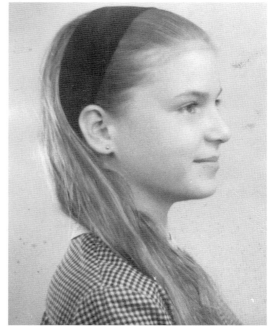

Mervyn and Maeve – last holiday, West Wittering, 1960.

(above) Fabian, Maeve and Mervyn – Drayton Gardens, 1963.

(below) Family at uncle's birthday party – London, 1963.

Maeve and Mervyn - in the gardens of the Priory, 1965.

Maeve painting in her studio – Drayton Gardens, 1968.

which briefly ebbed my flowing tears.

Our uniform was hideous. Everything I'd dreamed of in a school uniform was missing and it was one of the most disappointing experiences of my life. We stood in the Army & Navy Stores in Victoria with our mouths open, gazing at this despicable creation as they cruelly measured me for a life of ugliness for the next five years. I'd imagined it requisite that a boarding school would fit us out in a navy blue tunic with a square neck, pleats from the yoke, a tasselled, roped belt round the waist, a white shirt, and lisle stockings in the same colour as the tunic. Instead, I was being fitted with a V-neck, shitty brown, A-line dress, a beige shirt, brown tie, beige socks, a brown velour hat and a huge gingery brown coat that would keep me warm and mortified for years to come. I had visualised myself resembling a girl from St Trinian's, not a gruesome misfit from a school for plain girls who had no chance of a future boyfriend. I didn't know then what I know now, that it didn't matter what you wore, and that the chocolate-brown knickers up to the waist wouldn't put anyone off. The most attractive boys always fancied the girls from convent schools, regardless of what they were wearing.

So Maeve and her sister Matty took me back to the Surrey suburbs one sunny afternoon and left me at St Philomena's, a handsome convent school staffed entirely by nuns. With a brave face and painful Adam's apple, I waved goodbye to my aunt and mother and watched as their hire car wound round the drive and out of the gate, Maeve's waving hankie becoming smaller and smaller, until it had disappeared altogether. I was taken to the dining room and given a measly little plate of sandwiches filled with that foul invention, sandwich spread, and knew at once that I had made a terrible mistake. After the first term of sobbing into my pillow every night and writing home to let everyone know how deliriously happy I was, I settled down, and counted the days until I could go home for the weekend. Maeve sent me two postcards a week and by the time I left school, I had literally hundreds. She bought them from the Tate or the National Gallery, and the Matisses and Miros, Gauguins and Picassos, Goyas and Stanley Spencers, Klees and Rubens updated me on life at home. Her question, 'What do you think of this one?' would have me poring over the paintings, falling in love with some and left cold by others.

Do you like this one? Joan isn't a woman though, as you probably know. How is your collage going? I shall look forward to seeing it. Lots of love from Mum.

Darling, sorry not to have heard from you this week. Is your friend coming on Sunday? Sebby did another television advertisement the other day, but it won't be out for some time. Daddy is getting on as usual. Do you like this picture? The painter only painted on Sundays. Looking forward to seeing you so much. Love Mummy.

Mrs Peach has written to say she has finished your suit, and it looks very nice but she can't post it because of the 'go slow'. So I don't know when we will get it. Sebby left today. He didn't take his drums after all. We are going to dinner with Ronald Searle and his wife on Sunday. I'll see if I can get you an autographed drawing. Lots of love from Mummy.

My first school holiday home had me asking Maeve a

122

question that had bewildered me ever since Vincent had been born. Jill Browne, a nurse on *Emergency Ward Ten*, was having a baby. I knew she wasn't married and, like Carin, I couldn't understand how she'd managed to do this. 'Sit down and I'll explain,' my mother said in a proudly authoritative but faintly reticent voice. Despite being the daughter and sister, daughter-in-law and aunt of doctors, Maeve had scant (to say the least) knowledge on the workings of the human body. Technicalities on any subject were never a strong point, so her teaching of the facts of life were entirely idealistic.

'When you love someone, you want to show them how much you love them, and so you make love,' she said with a satisfied sigh. 'It's the most beautiful thing on earth, and nothing to be ashamed of.' She then went on to explain in a very rudimentary fashion the most astonishing thing I had ever heard. It didn't sound beautiful at all, it sounded utterly revolting, and I couldn't believe my parents had ever been capable of such deviant behaviour, blithely spending their days pretending to be normal. 'So I suspect Nurse Browne may have cared for the doctor,' she continued, 'and when you make love, sometimes you have a baby.' By the time I went back to school after the holidays everyone 'knew', and while comparing notes we agreed that the grown-up world was a very peculiar place indeed.

There were several sleeping blocks at school, some intimate four-bed annexes, and some long dormitories like a hospital ward. But what everyone waited for was their turn in the enormous, high-ceilinged six-bed room in the Queen Anne house beside the main school. It was majestic and elegant and had nothing whatsoever to do with boarding school. In this room we could take advantage of the privacy that came with being separate from the main buildings and do all the things we came to boarding school to do. We had midnight feasts and pillow fights, and we told ghost stories that went on long into the night. But most terrifying of all was the dare we devised for each other: the naked walk from the safety of our glorious room, down the wide, creaky staircase to the main door, past the sun-dial, and then the long walk into the black, shadowy grounds. Returning to the room without being caught by a nun or a murderer secured each other's ultimate respect.

In the dormitories, we had separate cubicles and in the mornings we stood to attention as our carefully made beds were stripped and pulled apart by the nuns, made, re-made and made again until our hospital corners were perfect. The nuns never missed an opportunity to intimidate or humiliate. I sustained no psychological damage, just a seething hatred for these petty, frustrated women. They were cold and distant, spiteful and uninteresting and not one of them made a good impression. I was one of the lucky ones, their bullying tactics didn't worry me in the least. I couldn't be hurt by people I had no respect for, and in the end they lost interest. But the vulnerable or lonely girls gave them just the thrill they were looking for. They taught cruelty well. We were ordered to put girls into coventry for insubordination, to ignore them as they sat at a table on their birthday and ate alone, to reject them if they cried. I refused to do this and was in constant trouble for leading mutinies against their nasty little rules.

At one end of the dormitory was the cell where a senior nun slept. It was bare of any comfort, with just a camp bed, a wooden chair and a massive crucifix hanging on the wall. For a while, in trouble yet again, I was consigned to a cubicle next door to the cell, and was convinced even my thoughts were being read through the thin plaster that divided us. It wasn't while I was in this cubicle but in the middle of the dormitory, with girls on either side of me, that odd things started happening. Someone was moving things around, clothes were leaving one girl's cubicle and making their way to another's. Family photographs were neatly stacked on bedside tables, personal belongings, letters, knickers, hair-brushes, soaps and school uniforms were finding themselves carefully arranged in the wrong cubicle.

We were all excited by this mystery. Apart from *Greengage Summer* being filmed at our school, nothing very stimulating happened at St Philomena's, other than crushes, and the occasional affair between sweet apostolate nuns, dressed in white and confused by loneliness and doubt in their 'calling'. Two of the nuns decided on a little covert surveillance and, one morning, I was called in to see Sister Superior to be informed that it was me. I was extremely upset to find I was responsible for this night-time madness, and I couldn't understand what was happening to me. I don't remember the reaction of my friends, but I do remember being taken to see our family doctor. He was wise and matter of fact. He was sure it was a reaction to what was happening at home. Subconsciously, I was muddled and needed some order to my thoughts, but waited until I was asleep for this. I was given a mild sleeping draught when I went back to school and the sleepwalking ceased entirely. Sleepwalking continued at home.

I wasn't unhappy at school. It was just that after home I found it so colourless. Sunday afternoons were spent rehearsing the Gay Gordon for future reels in Scottish castles, practising our back-straightening exercises in an unbroken circle around the assembly hall with a Bible on our heads, and perfecting our skills in 'alighting' from sports cars without showing our knickers. Our knees would be metaphorically glued together as we swiftly angled them to the left, daintily placed our toes, then heels to the floor, then stood up, briskly straightening our perfectly vertical backs in readiness for the chaste evening ahead with Sandy or Alistair.

Sadly, the nearest any of us got to a hint of romance were the crushes we had on each other. Friday night was music night when, for one blissful hour, we were allowed to play our own music on the record player and dance in the assembly hall. Our thoughts of young love were dreamily fantasised about with our arms around each other. The words to the songs were memorised easily, in a way no geography lesson could ever hope to be remembered. We were affected by every utterance, and learned everything we needed to know from the music we listened to. We were taken aback by the cavalier attitude of 'Twenty-four Hours to Tulsa', touched by the generosity of 'Take Good Care of my Baby', thrilled by 'Leader of the Pack', sobbed to 'Tell Laura I Love Her' and ached to be 'Runaround Sue'. The day girls had long gone home to their teas, their televisions, their fires and their families, and we had the school to ourselves. A lone nun sat rigidly on a hard-backed chair and observed us as we made the brave decision not to be unsettled by her disapproving looks and make the most of our one hour of abandon. Unfortunately, Elvis put a large spanner in the works. Much to the mystification of our more innocent souls, 'It's Now or Never' caused an outrage in the smutty minds of the nuns, so that dancing on a Friday night was banned. We huddled in corners while a 'big' girl clarified what 'be mine tonight' and 'my love can't wait' referred to, and what had once been a powerful love song now became some rapist's lament.

The girl I had a crush on was the most defiantly rebellious girl in the school. She was a louche and powerful loner, a couple of years above me, unafraid of the nuns and unafraid of her reputation as an oddity. She wore her dark hair in thick curly plaits and looked and acted like an even more insouciant Beryl the Peril. She was constantly in trouble and took her punishments with all the casualness of the truly brave. When she honoured me by asking me for a dance I was feted by all the girls. I had been singled out by one of the few truly original girls in the school; she became mine and I hers. Our crushes were pretty innocent affairs, but still to be taken very seriously, and having her on my side meant being bullied would never be on my agenda.

Fabian had met his future wife, Phyllida Barlow, at Chelsea Art School when I was twelve, and for a time at school their blossoming romance became the model against which all romance was gauged. I was quizzed at the beginning of every new term on the progress of their relationship, and when Fabian and Phyllida visited me or collected me at the end of a school term, girls hung from windows or followed me down the drive, hoping to catch a glimpse of this quasi-celebrity couple. Phyllida lived with her family in a huge, elegant house on Richmond Green, but 'Longacre', their house in Cley Next the Sea, Norfolk, is the place I remember best. Set behind a curved, flint wall, you walked through the black iron gates, past an avenue of sycamores, walnut trees and a croquet lawn, and there it was, facing you, this captivating house. Phyllida's father, Erasmus, was the great-grandson of Charles Darwin and Emma Wedgwood, and the house overflowed with their things. Ottoman ceramics and hand-painted china, ancient books and exotic birds peering out of tall glass cases, tiger skin rugs covering the stone floors, and strange and beautiful objects belonging to Erasmus and his lively and charismatic wife, Biddy. Every room was a feast of colour and texture. A million miles from interior design, it was effortlessly glamorous and original. Everything in the house had been arrived at naturally with no thought of mixing or matching, or suiting or not suiting, so there was no sense of contrivance. It was just a place of deep romance and entrancing atmosphere. The blood-red bathroom with its massive checkerboard floor had a huge sofa to recline on and, as your bath laboriously ran, you settled yourself down to read from one of the books pouring from the shelves.

Outside, leaning against the kitchen wall, were girl and boy bicycles, ranging in size, for the house-guests to borrow and ride around this lovely part of the world as the fancy took them. In the large kitchen beyond the informal dining room, Elena and I would sit with Biddy, shelling peas, and discussing anything and everything under the sun. In the evening, we'd sit nervously, listening to the erudite and often heated discussions taking place at the long refectory table. Just as frightening were the candle-lit stories that began at one end of the table and continued clockwise until every guest had had their turn, and the story had reached its ghostly or ghastly conclusion. It was terrifying and thrilling all at the same time. To my delight, one year, when I was twelve, I was seated opposite the Miranda of 'Do you remember an inn, Miranda?', the first line of Hilaire Belloc's poem 'Tarantella', which I knew well, and wanted to quiz her on, but I got the sense she had answered too many questions over the years. One evening, a few years later, when I had taken a boyfriend to 'Longacre', I cut my finger on the very sharp bread knife. Blood trickled down my hand and I fainted. Biddy called a doctor and the next thing I knew was finding myself lying in the most luxurious bed I have ever slept in, being given a once-over by him and a very worried-looking Biddy.

There were trips to Holkham Beach and Blakeney Point, where Erasmus and Biddy would team the guests for a game of cricket or rounders and, after a freezing swim, unravel the rugs for a picnic. Although only a member by proxy, I was always made to feel included in the truly extraordinary family Fabian had married into, and my childhood visits to Norfolk remain central to the memory of my adolescent years.

Seaside Songs

There were always semblances of normality, sterling attempts to live life like everyone else. On one or two occasions, Dad would join my mother and I on a family holiday to a lovely seafront hotel in West Wittering (oh, the glamour). My parents had never been adventurous travellers. Maeve became incredibly homesick about four miles out of central London, so our holidays never lasted for more than a week, and then the English south coast (the geographic equivalent of Swaziland) was travel enough. Although going home was what they were really looking forward to, we always had a wonderful time when we got there. It was just my parents and me – the boys were too old for family holidays – so the three of us walked on the beach, collected shells, slid on seaweed, sat on the sand letting the sea trickle between our toes, held hands and ran screaming into the grey water, made sandcastles, looked for crabs, sang songs, did the same thing every other family does on the English south coast. Such happy days!

In the evenings we dressed for dinner and the handsome Spanish waiters, hired for the summer season, made a fuss of me, while the band played unbearably touching songs, 'Begin the Beguine', 'Embraceable You', 'The Way You Look Tonight', and my father asked me to dance. I danced with him like I'd done when I was small, but he was uneasy. He stumbled and we stopped. Then my parents danced. I watched my mother as she held my father so he wouldn't fall. He was smiling; he looked happy. My mother caught my eye, blew me a kiss; her mouth was smiling but her eyes were dull with sadness. I watched the people as they watched my parents. Mervyn wanted to dance with his wife, he didn't see the people staring, he didn't see the nudging; for someone who spent his whole life noticing, he didn't hear the whispering. I saw the fascination on people's faces. What was this beautiful woman doing with this old man? Why was he shaking so. Why couldn't his feet make steps? Why did he look happy?

One summer we were asked to leave the hotel two days after we arrived. Dad was disturbing the other guests and upsetting their holidays. Again, too much optimism was to blame. We'd managed to convince ourselves there was a chance he might settle, but he couldn't. He paced the floor at night, he ran baths he forgot about, he offended guests when he tried to talk to them, he dribbled when he ate. So, with humiliated tears kept at bay, Mum and I packed our suitcases and made our way back home.

This last holiday coincided with my first period. I was eleven and we'd only just arrived at the hotel when it happened. I was extremely embarrassed, convinced the other guests could tell just by looking at me. I'd known this day was coming, but hadn't expected the pains that went with it. My stomach and my back ached and Maeve suggested I went to bed for the afternoon, where I fell into a

131

deep sleep. Dad, having been told I had the 'curse' for the first time, left the hotel and somehow found his way to the beach. He collected shells and pebbles and pieces of driftwood that he laid tenderly in a semi-circle at my feet and, without saying a word, walked out of the room, leaving me alone until we met at dinner.

Our holiday cut short, we returned to what we knew, Dad unable to sleep, Mum unable to sleep, night-time hours filled with disturbance. More unwatched baths left to stream, cigarettes left to burn through sofas, falling down, getting up, ambulances arriving, ambulances leaving, tears and reality. I had boarding school to run away to. I could escape to a world where only my best friends knew anything about my life at home. Maeve was left to cope with it all, and her insomnia was so acute she was hospitalised and sedated herself for a day or two. She told me her dreams had been extraordinary. I've forgotten them now.

While I was continuing with life at school, the mystery of Dad's illness continued. With one doctor contradicting another, it was difficult for Maeve to know what to do for the best. After being referred to, and having lengthy consultations with, a neurologist, it was decided that he have a lobotomy. It was such a huge decision for my mother to make but we all hoped fervently this would be the answer to all our prayers. I was at school on the day of the operation, while Maeve sat in a cinema watching, of all things, *Pollyanna*, seeing everything and seeing nothing, terrified the decision to operate would be the wrong one. The omens were already there. As she held her brother-in-law Lonnie's hand throughout the film, she failed to notice the man who sidled in next to her to steal the handbag sitting on the floor beside her, and in it the envelope with the money she kept safely by her side for the operation.

When I came home to see Dad for the first time after the operation, he looked utterly broken. I tried not to notice his shaved head or the desolation in his eyes because this was it, the thing that would have him leap-frogging over this chair at supper-time, the cure that would have him laughing at one of his own jokes. In the weeks that followed, a miracle occurred. Like grass sprouting from randomly strewn seeds, new hair began to appear. Standing up in confident little patches, it was soft as a baby's, and as I brushed the palm of my hand across his head it felt like hope.

It would take time, the doctors said, but eventually, with patience, we would notice a difference. The tremors would cease, the memory would return, the brain would begin to function properly, he would be well again. We *were* patient, but in the end when nothing changed, and things became only worse, we finally and reluctantly admitted defeat.

Van Gogh

Holidays became a thing of the past, something we never even thought about again. But when I was twelve I was invited by Sebastian to St Tropez to visit his best friend Oliver, who was running a hotel there. It can't have been a tempting proposition for Sebastian, aged twenty-two. All I planned from my trip was a glimpse of Brigitte Bardot, and a gingham bikini, one of which I managed to achieve. One night we drove to Juan Les Pins to see Nina Simone at an open-air concert. Arriving early so as to secure front-row seats, there was a hush of expectant silence as she was introduced. As we waited for the first note to be delivered, she slowly scanned the audience. There was a heavy silence, we waited, she looked again, we tried to look less uninspiring – we failed. 'I don't like you,' she spat as she turned her back on us and walked off the stage and we, the puzzled and disappointed audience, collected our belongings and returned from whence we came.

I found my gingham bikini in a minute boutique. Positioning the tiny top over my gnat bite of a bosom, I eased the bottom half over my knickers to the enthusiastic urgings ('Oh! You must get it') of the only other person in the ultra-modern communal changing room – Virginia McKenna.

Back at school I passed the tedious days having imaginary friendships with famous people. I wrote poems to and about them, all of them sincere, all of them dreadful. None of these people were alive and not one of them an original person to love. I was in a fan club of millions, but still they spoke to me in a way that moved me profoundly. There was John Clare, Van Gogh and Marilyn Monroe, Oscar Wilde, Edith Piaf and Billie Holiday, James Dean, Emily Brontë and A. E. Housman, all unashamedly passionate and sensitive and precisely what I was looking for in this land of the unmoved.

After lights out I shone my torch under my bedclothes and read Vincent's letters to Theo and cried myself to sleep imagining his life, his wonderful brother, his roughly formed face, his orange beard, his thick, expressive paint, his lonely mission, his bed, his lack of love. The pure emotion that surged through my body made it impossible to look at one of his pictures without hot tears slipping down my face. I wanted to tell him that at thirteen I didn't need to be told he was good, that every fibre of my body reacted to his pictures all by itself. And although I didn't know it at the time, my father must have felt exactly the same.

VAN GOGH

Dead, the Dutch Icarus who plundered France
And left her fields the richer for our eyes.
Where writhes the cypress under burning skies,

135

Or where proud cornfields broke at his advance,
Now burns a beauty fiercer than the dance
Of primal blood that stamps at throat and thighs.
Pirate of sunlight! and the laden prize
Of coloured earth and fruit in summer trance
Where is your fever now? and your desire?
Withered beneath a sunflower's mockery,
A suicide you sleep with all forgotten.
And yet your voice has more than words for me
And shall cry on when I am dead and rotten
From quenchless canvases of twisted fire.

I lay in bed and learned great chunks of 'The Ballad of Reading Gaol' and 'A Shropshire Lad'. I read *Wuthering Heights* and imagined I was Cathy, running to the moor, waiting for Heathcliff to find me, as torrential rain lashed at my pallid face. I dreamed of Marilyn. Giggling side by side, wads of cotton wool separating our crimson toenails, our hair curled in gigantic rollers, a silk scarf tied around our alien-like heads, we chatted together. I found a garish copy of *Lady Sings the Blues* at home, which told me some of the facts of Billie Holiday's short and troubled life and, at the time, I thought everything I read about her as imperative as the music I listened to over and over again. If this now seems overly romantic, I'm not embarrassed. The adults surrounding me day in and day out were ordinary and un-mysterious in the extreme; even their passion for Jesus seemed obscured by an aggressive thirst for the prosaic.

After holidays, it was back to school – back to the grindingly tedious suffering for our sins, the constant praying for the less fortunate, the endless waiting for every other Sunday to arrive, the early morning train to Victoria

Station and freedom. I could almost feel the shackles falling away as the train pulled into the station and I searched under the clock to see which member of my family would be there to greet me. It was almost worth going to boarding school for that day every fortnight, when you could shed the dreary conversation of the nuns, shake off the constant reminder of the mortal and venial sins you'd no doubt committed, and escape the aridity and putrid smell of pretend goodness. The Sunday morning bustle of the tube – the gorgeous London air, the coffee at Dino's and the slow walk up the Old Brompton Road to the heavenly warmth of our basement kitchen.

Dad came home occasionally and sometimes his weekend coincided with mine. By now it was becoming impossible to understand anything he said, which was just as frustrating for him as for everyone else, but we were all there to help him, and his inherent playfulness was impossible to extinguish. We would put a record on and he would do a funny little dance to make us laugh, and attempt to imitate Groucho's walk. He had always been so supple and athletic, leap-frogging over his chair at meal-times, running up the down escalators at the station, the simplest and most ordinary thing made fun, and still he tried.

There are a few similarities between us, small tics that tell me I am my father's daughter. But for them, it would be hard to believe we were related. His eyes were blue, mine are green; he was tall, I'm small; he was dark, I'm fair; he was thin, I'm round. I hadn't inherited any of his talent, but I had inherited his cheerful disposition, his squeamish temperament and his propensity to faint. Mervyn's most memorable faint was when he slid down a wall while being measured for his army uniform, assuming he was being measured for his coffin. We both found it impossible not to pass out when doctors squeezed our arm into a sausage for a blood-pressure reading. Just the sound of the air breathing in and out was enough to do it for both of us.

My fainting fits began at school, when the long silences in our daily Mass and Sunday Benediction gave me the time to imagine myself transported to another time and place – a forgiving place, where the constant worry of having committed a mortal sin could be alleviated, without the fear and humiliation of unburdening it to our school priest. Surely he must have recognised our voices and stored up our smutty little secrets, held us in contempt for the dreadful interior life we were leading. I hated the feeling just before I slid down the tiny, cramped space between kneeling and sitting on the hard benches, the spinning head, the clammy hands, the humiliation. The relief after we had taken con-fession, when we were clean again, had earned a fresh start – no more dirty thoughts, no more swear words carved into desks, no more imagining what it would be like to be kissed, no more hatred for the nuns. It could all be wiped out with the simple words: 'Bless me Father, for I have sinned.'

The early 1960s had seminal moments and, like everyone else, I remember them well. A sunny lunch with Mary Norton in her daughter's garden was abruptly interrupted when Sebastian ran out of her kitchen to tell us Marilyn Monroe had died. My head was bent over a sink in the communal washroom as a screaming sixth former came running in to tell us the news of Kennedy's assassination. Her jumbled words were incomprehensible through my shampooed ears but, as I looked up from the washbowl, soap pouring down my face, I saw groups of girls huddled together, wailing uncontrollably as only groups of girls can

138

wail. As we tacked the Broderie Anglaise frill around our crisp white aprons, a song burst on to the radio in our warm sewing class. It was 'Love Me Do' by The Beatles. Our response was immediate. We'd never heard anything like it before and, in those few short minutes, each and every one of us was smitten. For us, and every other thirteen-year-old girl in the country, it was the start of Beatlemania. It was 1963.

Two Cinemas in One Street

Our house was at one end of a terrace, and halfway down sat the Paris Pullman, a stylish and intimate little cinema where foreign and classic films of a heavier-than-average weight were shown. If your tastes leant towards the popular, you only had to cross the street, walk a few yards and there was the Fulham Forum, a fat and comfortable flea-pit, where many a rainy afternoon was spent enjoying the B movie before the main feature reeled its way into my consciousness. For a film fan, two cinemas in one street was luxury beyond belief; I could see everything I wanted, classic and contemporary, foreign and Hollywood, appalling and inspirational. One Easter holiday I went to the Paris Pullman to see *East of Eden* for the first time. I was so moved by James Dean's performance that I went to see it over and over again that holiday. I silently mouthed every syllable that Jo Van Fleet, Raymond Massey, Julie Harris, James Dean, Richard Davalos and Burl Ives uttered, and was horrified by Raymond Massey's insensitive treatment of his son, Cal. Never has a film so accurately exposed the pain of a child rejected by a parent, and the lengths that child will go to win a parent's love.

James Dean's portrayal was flawless, and it didn't matter how many times I saw the film, I still ached with the injustice of it all.

Later, Sebastian took me to see *Les Enfants du Paradis*, and this time I left the Paris Pullman overwhelmed and in love. My previous crush had been harder to understand. Mike Winters, the marginally more handsome brother of Bernie, had given me many a sleepless night, and when I switched my affections to Jean Louis Barrault, although puzzled by my own eclecticism, I recognised this as a turning point to a more discerning change of heart. I loved his ethereal and idiosyncratic quality, and if we'd been the same age when the film came out, I would have swum the English Channel and made him mine. Instead, I wrote him a letter and sent it to the Comédie Française. A month later a special delivery postman handed me a single pink rose with a letter attached. The letter, carried around with me in every pocket of every coat and eventually lost when it fell out on the water slide at Battersea funfair, told of his joy on receiving my letter, of his wish I consider myself his 'Little Arletty' in London, of his hope my life was a full and happy one. It was a generous and perceptive letter and I treasured it, along with his rose, which stood for a while in a vase of constantly replenished water until the petals had all fallen off and the lonely stalk didn't seem worth saving. He invited me to visit him at the Comédie Française. I never went.

Back at school the tedious days rolled on, one ordinary day the same as the next. We went 'down the field' and lay on the grass with our blue-and-white striped summer dresses tucked tightly between our legs – 'There are work-men here, girls, cover yourselves up' – and talked for hours about the boys 'out there' who would be our husbands. We all vowed to be virgins when we married, and I think one of us was. One night someone sneaked some cigarettes into the dormitory and we all piled into my cubicle, like Jack Lemmon in *Some Like It Hot*. But lacking the essential member of the opposite sex, all we could do was draw deeply on our individual cigarette, perfect our inhalation skills and elegantly throw our wrists back à la Bette Davis. We were just discussing the boys out there and 'how far' we would go with them when one of the nuns pulled my curtain open with such force that it tore off its rings. 'As from tomorrow you are suspended,' she screamed, 'but first you will have a meeting with Sister Superior, and finally you'll be sent home, where you will have your parents to deal with.'

Sister Superior looked me up and down with her pince-nez perched on the tip of her absurdly hooked nose. 'Clare Peake,' she said, as if I were a clod of muck she'd spotted on the sole of her shiny, wrinkled shoe. 'You are C.O.M.M.O.N – VULGAR!' It seemed such a curious thing to say. I expected to be punished, I deserved it, but I'd never thought of myself as common or vulgar, and the spelling of 'common' letter by letter struck me as very odd. But 'Clare Peake you are c.o.m.m.o.n. – vulgar' became one of those delicious family in-jokes, treasured forever, and rolled out every time I did anything wrong.

I met my mother under the clock at Victoria Station, where we both went along with her stab at stunned outrage for a fraction of a second, then got down to the real business of enjoying the next seven days of our lovely unplanned week together. We saw *The Miracle Worker* and *The Loneliness of the Long Distance Runner*, we strolled to Kensington Gardens to visit Peter Pan for the millionth time, we went to the Tate to

142

be thrilled yet again by the Picassos, and we went to buy a bra. As my bosom had begun to grow into something resembling the real thing, it was time to take it seriously, so off we trotted to Peter Jones so I could be fitted for a first bra by one of their formidable lady measurers. With the tape wound around her neck, and my shivering bosom hoping to make a good impression, we finally settled for the 'Dawn Bra' – 'A lovely snug fit, young lady'. We then looked for grown-up clothes to complement my new shape.

This was a never-to-be-forgotten day, spent trying on whole outfits from the inside out – not children's clothes but thrilling, earth-shattering ensembles. First there was an up-to-the-minute polo-neck jumper, and through the thin black wool, my twin bosoms were so high and pointed they could easily have poked a small man's eyes out. Then an orange corduroy shift dress, black stockings and suspender belt, patent leather shoes with a kitten heel and, finally and most thrilling of all, my first bottle of perfume – Chanel No. 5. What else? The scent Marilyn wore. I'd never been spoilt, so this experience was too wonderful for words. As I stood staring at myself in the full-length mirror, I felt ready to face the world with shy equanimity. Just one more thing was needed to make my transformation complete. After enormous deliberation, I had my dead straight, waist-length hair cut into a tight just-below-the-ears perm and, in one fell swoop, I went from modern teenage girl to middle-aged accounts manager.

There was a reason for my new look. I was being taken to see *Two Stars for Comfort*, the new John Mortimer play at the Garrick. Maeve's great friend, Esmond Knight, was in it, and we were going backstage to say hello to him, and for me to be introduced to Trevor Howard, the star of the production. I'd seen *Brief Encounter* on television one Sunday afternoon and, of course, knew exactly who he was. Was he primed? I didn't think so at the time, but as we entered his dressing room he gasped, 'Oh hello, you gorgeous girl. How wonderful to meet you. Now how old did your mother say you were. No, don't tell me, you must be fifteen or is it sixteen?' 'I'm thirteen,' I whispered, my new bosom heaving like a real woman's. 'Well, I simply can't believe it,' he said. I looked at Maeve who nodded in agreement. 'Do you think I might take you out to dinner when you are eighteen, if your mother lets me? Now don't forget will you?' 'No, I won't,' I said, floating out of that theatre on air. What a little charm can do!

Because Esmond looked you straight in the eye, it was impossible to believe he couldn't see you. A classical leading man, he was on his way to becoming a major star when, in 1941, on HMS *Prince of Wales*, an exploding shell blinded him in one eye and partially blinded him in the other. His complete lack of self-pity had he and I regularly playing marbles with his glass eye. Out it popped and was added to the beautiful, opaque, vein-threaded marbles Dad had brought home from China. After the game was over, I would hunt for it, he would pretend to hunt for it, a quick dust and back it was popped.

Esmond was one of the kindest men I ever met, and I was immensely fond of him. Cuddling up to him on the sofa, I would ask, and he would tell me, over and over again, what I wanted to hear about Marilyn Monroe. 'Tell me again Es,' I would say, and he would, as though it were the very first time. He had worked with her on *The Prince and the Showgirl* and, although he liked her very much, like so many before him, he said she could be infuriating to work with. Sensing my disappointment, he always added that her adorable charm made it impossible to be cross for long. Then, attempting to hide his boredom, he went on to describe in detail her skin, her clothes, her height, her weight, her laugh, until at last we were interrupted and poor Esmond was finally allowed some peace.

Maeve's little joke, 'How can you tell a bore? Ask them how they are and they tell you,' stood her in good stead. It wasn't actually true, she was immensely sympathetic, but was absolutely of the 'get on with it' generation, who had gone through a war and learned the hard way that things sometimes got better if you didn't talk about them. Finding it such a bore to talk about her own troubles may have been one of the reasons she was always so popular, and her friends remained the same friends until the day she died. Every year there were a few additions, handsome young poets and dashing young editors, who arrived as fans of Mervyn's and became friends with Maeve. Paul Chown, a young librarian at the Westminster Library, remembered her. 'It was always gin, which she could never remember, or perhaps quite believe, that I didn't like, and a lump of cheese cut into little squares. I think I began to believe she lived on gin and cheese. I would have believed anything: it was all magic to me.'

Michael Moorcock arrived at the house in Surrey when I was seven and he was a seventeen-year-old fan of Mervyn's. He was the same age as Sebastian and Fabian but, although I was a child and he an incredibly talented and hardworking teenager, he always took notice. His deep affection for my parents and theirs for him has been a constant backdrop to my life, and I think of him as an extension of our family. He's always been there, a support, an ally and a friend, and the first person I rang after Maeve died.

When I was fourteen, he asked whether I would like to play 'The Girl' in a film he was writing and directing, a role, I think, intrinsic to the whole movie. I was picked up early every morning and spent the next few weeks wandering around a bomb-site in Ladbroke Grove, feeling unbearably self-conscious. But Michael was endlessly encouraging. 'Fantastic work, Clare,' he'd say, as 'wooden' took on a new dimension, far beyond the realms of Stanislavski's darkest nightmare. I don't know what happened to the film, I never saw it, but somewhere out there, coiled in a circular tin, on a dusty shelf, in some unknown room are reels showing a brown-haired girl in a black duffel coat, standing stiff as a cricket bat and mute as – a mute.

Books to Change a Life

The school terms traipsed wearily on, but when I reached fourteen the discovery of adult books changed everything. On a Friday night, the books trolley could be heard clanking along on its rollers, stopping sharply at the closed-curtained cubicle of each girl, like a nurse doing the rounds with the medicine. There was no dawdling, we had to choose chop-chop, so it could be rather a hit or miss affair. As you were hastily choosing the book that would, with any luck, overwhelm your senses for the coming week, a nun would dart her beady eye around your cubicle, searching for any sign of aberration, an un-emptied wash-bowl, a forbidden comic, a wet towel.

The first grown-up book I read was *The Ordeal of Gilbert Pinfold*, and I was absolutely knocked out by it. My eyes were opened to a different kind of writing and I understood, or thought I understood, Gilbert Pinfold's slide into hallucination and madness. The intense Catholicism of him and his wife, the voices he heard, the confusion he experienced, it all seemed so familiar, and if this was the world of adult literature, I wanted more. A stream of perfect books gave my heart exactly what it was searching for, and

147

a captivating first sentence could almost send me into a trance. I wanted to coil up in the imagery, let the words take me to places I'd never been to before. *The Constant Nymph*, *The Well of Loneliness*, *Cold Comfort Farm*, *The Green Carnation*, *Trilby*, *Liza of Lambeth*, *Love in a Cold Climate*, *Three Men in a Boat*, *The Sign of the Four* and my father's favourite book of all time, *The Diary of a Nobody*, allowed me this luxury. Some of the titles managed to slip through the net, and had the nuns known the subject matter of a few, there would have been some late-night sacrificial burning, I'm sure. Many of the books were hagiographies and I read my fair share. It was always so hard to resist a grotto. Although the lives of the saints never remained in my thoughts in the same way that characters from pure literature did, St Theresa and St Francis had all the qualities I had naively thought our nuns would possess.

Besides reading, my other overriding passion was Ray Charles. I was crazy about his music and went to see him every time he played the Hammersmith Odeon, his usual haunt. I always went on my own, but I didn't mind that, or standing at the back, as I usually did. In fact, I preferred it. He and the Raelettes gave electrifying performances and by the time 'Georgia on my Mind' or 'You Don't Know Me' closed the show, I was floating away (in the words of Ellen Gilchrist) in a land of dreamy dreams.

Sunday, that cruellest of days, gloomy enough when you're happy, but quadrupled when you're sad. Well, the depression of an early Sunday evening at boarding school is worse. We did our homework, wrote to our families and turned the assembly hall into a cinema where we watched the same films over and over again: *The Nun's Story*, *The Song of Bernadette*, *Carve Her Name with Pride*, *The Inn of the Sixth*

Happiness, anything they could dig up with a 'holy' theme. Sometimes we went on school outings. As the coach passed near my house on the way to the Science Museum, the Natural History Museum or the V&A, I nearly went mad with the frustration at being so close to freedom but unable to escape.

While I was only faintly aware of financial difficulties, Maeve's life was one of continual struggle. The Artist's Benevolent Fund was a great help and sent me birthday cards and thoughtful little presents, and contributed towards my upkeep when things became really tough. Friends and admirers of Mervyn's offered to help. Elizabeth Bowen, Iris Murdoch and Brigid Brophy suggested initiating a fund, persuading other writers to join them in helping my parents with the astronomical bills the hospitals charged when National Health Service hospitals refused to keep him any more, because there was nothing more they could do for him. Maeve, though deeply touched, found it impossible to accept money she knew she would never be able to repay. She got by, selling her own and Mervyn's work, and spent day after day, year after year, trying to get Mervyn's books republished. Agents discouraged her. The time had gone, they said. There was no market for Mervyn Peake any more. But the perspicacity of Michael Moorcock, his wife Hilary Bailey, their great friend Langdon Jones and Oliver Caldicott, the far-sighted editor of Penguin Books, paid off. Penguin Modern Classics republished the *Titus* books and a generation living through the sixties discovered Mervyn all over again.

I was now dressing in the uniform of the day – dove grey

149

pencil skirt, flesh-coloured stockings, patent leather sling-backs and white frilly pirate blouse. I don't think I've ever felt so great as I did then. It was wonderful to be alive, wonderful to be a girl, wonderful to be my parents' daughter, wonderful to be a Londoner. Life was now beginning in earnest. I had given up my dancing lessons at Madame Vacani's in Knightsbridge, trading them in for the afternoon sessions at the Streatham Locarno, which seemed sexier and filled with more possibility. The girls wore their dolly rocker dresses and the boys their mohair suits, and slow dancing to Smokey Robinson on a shiny dance floor was always going to be a more thrilling experience than waltzing on parquet to the strains of Victor Silvester. The West End was within walking distance, and I spent my school holidays in the Macabre coffee bar in Dean Street, where beatniks sat on coffins drinking black coffee, and my nights in the Café des Artistes, where edgy boys from the World's End tried to take advantage, and Eel Pie Island, where I saw Alexis Korner and the Yardbirds, among so many others. Sebastian took me to Ronnie Scott's, the Marquee and the Flamingo Club, and, at fourteen, years younger than anyone else, I loved mingling with the jazz aficionados in their black polo-neck jumpers and the gorgeous girls who all looked like Juliette Greco or Françoise Hardy. I loved listening to the complex music wafting from shiny instruments, and bouncing sweet melodies off the wall.

As most of my friends' families lived overseas, I brought a different girl home to stay on every other weekend visit; otherwise they never left the school. In the holidays, when they returned to Hong Kong or Germany or Cyprus or wherever their fathers were based, and if Elena wasn't staying, I went out alone or with my new friend Nichola, a year or so above me at school but the only other girl who lived in central London. A clever and urbane girl, she and I would have enormous fun when I got to sixteen or so. She would take me dancing to West Indian clubs in Bayswater and Notting Hill, and in the holidays secured me a job at the Golden Egg in Hammersmith, where we waitressed together. My mother came in to see me there, silently clapping and mouthing 'Oh well done' every time I took another Golden Brunch to a customer. I went to Barnes church hall dances, where we did the twist and the shake, heads moving frantically, hair mussing to perfection, gleaming white knee-length socks keeping their elasticity, as cool, unsmiling boys from St Paul's looked on. I went to the Chelsea Town Hall dances, where we danced to ska and blue beat, and the older boys and girls took purple hearts, and I spent most of my evening fending off the ugly boy. There was always one; he was generic: he stood alone, and something infuriatingly perceptive told him that, after having been refused by the prettiest girls in the room, I wouldn't have the heart to say no. I couldn't live with the guilt of watching the heart-breaking walk back to his lonely corner.

Then there was Battersea funfair, a short stroll over Albert Bridge, that prettiest bridge in the world, sixpence at the turnstile and a longing gaze at the boy on the rifle range. He was the most beautiful creature I had ever laid eyes on, more beautiful than Marlon Brando or James Dean, and I found myself becoming very adept at the old rifle, my eye trained to within feet of landing that stuffed panda. We eventually got talking and when I shyly admitted I was fourteen and at convent boarding school, there was a noticeable pricking to

151

his ears. Unable to comprehend my sudden appeal, but nevertheless thrilled, we became pen-pals. He wrote requesting trivial details of my day-to-day life in a convent boarding school, and then thorough descriptions of my friends, finally enquiring about the precise location of my school, because he and his friends were going to scale the wall and spend some time with us.

Only two of my friends had the guts to join me, so the three of us waited one freezing night until we saw the impossibly thrilling sight of 'boys' jumping twenty feet into our arms. The nuns had been snoring peacefully for hours and somehow I didn't care any more if I was caught. He and his friends weren't exactly what you would describe as boys; all were in their twenties and extremely sure of themselves. We had been asked specifically to wear our school uniforms and, after leading them to the gym as requested, they sat and smoked cigarettes and watched us silently as we climbed the ropes with our dresses tucked into the back of our knickers. After mumbling a desultory goodbye they scaled the wall, out of our school and out of our lives, without having uttered a single word. What strange creatures boys were, and what, I now realise, a lucky escape we had.

I still longed to be at home, or anyway not a boarder. The day girls were growing up in a way we weren't, and the gap between us was widening fast. While we boarders were still getting our thrills from listening to Radio Luxembourg after lights out, praying that Pete Murray might dedicate another song to the girls in our dorm, they had proper dates with boys. They bought make-up and experimented with blue eye shadow, they teased their hair into bee-hives, they wore stockings and frilly suspender belts under their brown tunics, and they learnt new dances. They talked of their bodies in sections – no-go areas and free-houses. There was a whiff of emancipation in the air and we were being left behind, cooped up, on the shelf. I wanted a boyfriend. I wasn't prepared to wait any longer.

I lived too far from school, so I went to live at Elena's and became a day girl myself. I knew the family well and was made to feel completely at home, but the rules were strict at Elena's and, not keen on being dispatched back to boarding school, I toed the line in most of the ways expected of me. Elena (a desperado in the making) was not so compliant but, in her own house, free to rebel as much as she wanted. Like everyone else of our age, we had started smoking. The five Capstan full-strengths we bought every morning were enough to last the day. We smoked one each on the way to school and one each on the way home, which left one to share on our early evening homework break. We knew we were too young to be smoking, but in those days the only harmful side-effect anyone warned you about was stunted growth.

Everyone with a cigarette in their mouths seemed to be of perfectly average height, we ourselves had grown to a normal height, so it was hard to understand the spluttering fury that overcame Elena's mother when she discovered us casually puffing on our well-earned cigarette, aiming the smoke out of our bedroom window. By a stroke of coincidence, Elena's father chose that precise moment to enjoy an innocent (or was it?) meander around his unlit garden. Although we couldn't see him, annoyingly he could see us, or not us exactly but the perfectly formed smoke rings blowing northwards, in the direction of his quietly pacing body. Our punishment was to be the cruellest blow anyone

153

could inflict on two young girls at the height of Beatlemania. Our precious tickets to a Beatles concert were to be confiscated until after the show, tickets we had embraced every night for weeks. Instead, we were to endure the ignominy of listening to every detail of the Fab Four's performance second-hand from our hoarse and unbearably smug school friends. On the night of the concert, as they stood screaming, sobbing and holding their heads in abandon, Elena and I sat on her bed and plotted.

Tickets for a forthcoming Royal Albert Hall concert had been sold out months before but, as we were to be seeing them locally, we hadn't bothered to try for this more celebrated venue. It was impossible to contemplate being left behind while the rest of the country talked about what it felt like to be sitting in the same space and breathing the same air as The Beatles. They occupied our thoughts, the same as they occupied the thoughts of every other nubile girl in Great Britain. I had bullied my mother into learning all four names from a massive poster I had pinned to my wall. To the uninitiated, they had more than a hint of the doppelganger, with the Beatle mops, collarless suits and cheeky grins, and it took time, but with my chop-stick at the ready I pointed them out again and again until I could be certain that she could tell at a glance the difference between John and Paul, George and Ringo. Arbitrary spot checks from other sources were thrust under her nose, so I could be sure that we weren't just playing a guessing game and she really knew. Her bored little face showed signs of relief when she had finally cracked it, but this brainwashing didn't pay off in the long run as I found to my chagrin a couple of years later when I forced her to sit silently on my bed for as long as an album takes to play and listen to Bob Dylan. She'd had enough, and 'Desolation Row' would never be listened to with the reverence I knew it deserved.

We didn't stand a hope in hell of getting tickets for the Royal Albert Hall, but we knew that, at some time during the day, The Beatles would be contained in all their wonderfulness fifteen minutes from where I lived. That Sunday morning, before the crack of dawn, Elena and I crept out of my house and made our way to the Albert Hall. We hid in a side entrance, perfecting our northern accents and waiting to ambush anyone who might be able to help. Eventually, a doorman arrived. With dreadful northern enunciation we informed him that we had hitchhiked all the way from Leeds for a chance to meet our idols. He listened patiently, and either his ear wasn't very good or our accents were better than we thought, because he offered to help. Following him up endless steps, we settled down in the back row of the upper circle, out of view, or so we thought. He had asked us to sit quietly until The Beatles arrived to rehearse, and then it was up to us how we went about introducing ourselves. If one of us had only paid more attention in sewing class, the present we had brought might not have shamed us quite so much. 'Beatle Baby' was an unpleasant little creation made from dusty pink satin and filled with cotton wool and old stockings. It had floppy arms and legs, huge ears, a long and static tail (a knitting needle had been thrust through its bottom and kept it rigid) and it looked nothing like a beetle but quite like an udder. Our plan was to hand it to them, then disappear.

We dozed in our seats for a couple of hours, until we were sharply awakened by the blare of guitar tuning and vocal limbering by what looked from the distance like five pretty girls. Training my suddenly alert eye on the stage, I spotted a haircut on one of them that took my fancy. We found a sixpence, retrieved some binoculars and took it in turns to watch the group as their rehearsal got going. It suddenly hit us that these weren't five pretty girls, but five pretty boys. These were The Rolling Stones, and it was Brian Jones' bob that I thought I might replicate.

The playing stopped sharply as they looked up and noticed us. A friendly Mick Jagger called us down to explain ourselves. 'We're waiting to meet The Beatles, give them a present and be on our way,' we said. 'Waiting for The Beatles, eh? What are you waiting for The Beatles for? We're going to be as big as The Beatles soon and we're here,' Mick said. I went to find a telephone to let my mother know we were both safe, but wouldn't be joining her at the Brompton Oratory as planned, when suddenly the phone was snatched from my hand. 'Mum, she won't be going to Mass today. She's with us, we'll look after her, OK?' said Mick Jagger. I turned around and there they were, standing right next to me, Elena chatting away to John Lennon as though she had known him all her life. In all her maturity, she had always fancied John the most. 'You know how you can tell he's married,' she had said. 'Have a good look at his legs next time you see him on the telly and you'll notice they're always parted.'

Until a few hours later when Susan Maugham, Kenny Lynch, the Fentones and various other artistes turned up to rehearse, we had The Beatles and The Rolling Stones all to ourselves. Our Beatle Baby went down a storm and, as I sat on John Lennon's lap, he threaded the tail between my legs and everyone laughed as he made comments that I didn't understand and gamely joined in my nervous giggling. Elena and I swapped laps, so that she sat on John's and I sat on Paul's, and we began to think we were dreaming. Luckily, I'd remembered to bring my autograph book with me. Someone (the doorman?) had called the press, and we were interviewed, photographed and made the front page of a now-lost magazine. Mick, Keith, John and Paul (and, less feverishly, the others) tried hard to get us tickets, but it was impossible. They kissed us goodbye, waved us off at the stage door and, as we fought our way through the crowds of lucky people who did have tickets, Elena and I looked at each other and laughed. We had pulled it off, and we returned to school as stars, our exploit ensuring our immense popularity for a good week after that. We did eventually see The Beatles performing and, although I promised myself I wouldn't, I couldn't help myself – like every other girl in the auditorium, I screamed from the moment they arrived on the stage to the moment they left.

First Love

I left school with an insouciant shrug and no backward wave, never to be visited and, until now, never to be thought of again. The years had passed, it was 1964, I was almost sixteen and the world was at my feet. Dad was now at the Priory Hospital in Roehampton, an absurdly expensive place, but a place that would, at least, keep him when other hospitals refused. I hated it there. The beauty of the grounds couldn't disguise the surliness of the staff or the look of torpor in the patients. Odd that a place so handsome and held in such high esteem should make me sadder than other hospitals I'd visited him in over the years. I don't know what it was; it just felt lonelier.

Another anonymous gift of money dropped through the letter box – an amount that could guarantee a few more months in this fashionable sanatorium. This time Lonnie was suspected. Maeve visited three times a week, and I went whenever I felt able. Like everything else, there had never been any pressure to do so. Guilt had never been used as a weapon and it wouldn't start now. But the visits were becoming almost too painful. I searched for a sign of recognition. I was his daughter; surely he would know me.

But he never did – I was just a stranger who held him too tight and kissed him too hard. I sat on his lap, stroking the stubble of his roughly shaved cheek, inhaling deeply, as always, his smell being the only sense I could still rely on not to alter. To leave him unloved and uncared for by this team of disinterested staff was more than I could bear, so as I walked away I erased the images, cowardly banishing them from my mind until my next visit.

I met my first boyfriend at a party when I was living at Elena's. I was just fifteen and he was eighteen, and we knew from that very first meeting that we were in for the long haul. There had been lots of semi-boyfriends, but nobody I felt was my very own until Frank, this quiet, handsome, political boy, talked to me about the book he was reading. We sat shyly side by side on a sofa as he related the story of *Crime and Punishment*, of Raskolnikov, of the old woman, of his experiment. All around us, boys and girls kissed and drank and, as he took my hand in his, I fell in love for the first time. He was grown-up and experienced, and he knew that I wasn't, and so we found a room to be alone in and talked until dawn.

We met a week later, but this time was more difficult. I met some of his friends, a group who appeared much older than I was, and desperately world-weary. A plain, sneering girl looked down her nose at me and cockily asked everyone present, 'Who's never been depressed here, then?' Before I had time to think, my arm shot up and she sniggered, 'Umm, I thought so. Don't you know that to be even remotely interesting or intelligent you have to know depression?' 'No,' I answered, 'I didn't.' Not long afterwards, I contracted a particularly virulent strain of glandular fever and became very ill and extremely depressed but never discovered the luxury of 'feeling remotely interesting or intelligent'.

It took a long time to recover and, as the days became brighter, Mum and I played games together. The alphabet game, naming books, flowers, films, poets, painters, animals, trees, emotions, traits, diseases, rivers, countries, cities, towns, from A–Z. We played Pelmanism, which I won every time, and she read me *The Napoleon of Notting Hill* and short stories by Colette and Saki. On the day I was to get up for the first time I felt worse than ever. I had lost a lot of weight and I looked tired and ill, but worse than that was the depression, which was deepening and frightening and opaque. A dreadful malaise had set in and I didn't know this person I'd become. I lay in bed as tears streamed incessantly. Back came Dr Roberts to diagnose mumps on one side. Two weeks later, the other side blew up. Day in, day out, I existed on tiny, crustless cheese and pickle sandwiches, which I sucked, an orange, peeled and arranged around the plate like the sun, and a small Milky Way. I couldn't stomach anything else. Eventually, I was well enough to get up, but during the weeks that I'd been ill, the outside world had changed. It smelt of something I didn't recognise. There was a brittle reality that had somehow eluded me before. London looked bleak and judgemental and I wanted to go back to sleep forever. I had been in one room for too long. Nothing was serious, nothing I wouldn't recover from, but there was a subtle change in the air and I didn't like it. I had lived in boarding school or Elena's for too long. I wasn't used to being at home all the time and everything felt strangely unfamiliar.

But still, anything was better than school, or minding my p's and q's in someone else's house. There was so much family life to catch up on, and to be free of the inevitable constraints of school was heaven. I had by now dyed my hair platinum blonde; I could at least have the same colour as Marilyn. The barely diluted peroxide was daringly combed through by Elena, so that overnight the condition of my hair went from thick and brown to thin and yellow, but at least from now on I would always be described as blonde. My boyfriend had left home and instead of cycling nightly from Surrey to see me had found himself a room in Earl's Court, so we could be within walking distance of each other and be together whenever we wanted, which was all the time. Maeve, a realist, had come timidly into my room late one night. 'If you need to see Dr Roberts about anything, feel free. He's expecting your call.' She didn't want to discuss my personal life, I didn't want to discuss my personal life; we weren't best friends, we were mother and daughter but, like all truthful and realistic mothers, she knew what was going on. She'd cleverly arranged it with a minimum of embarrassment and a maximum of pragmatism that I get myself sorted out. It must have been hard for someone of her generation, but it was far better to be sensible than pregnant, and, anyway, I suspect she had never seen making love with someone you love as anything other than natural.

In the school holidays I had worked at the Troubadour coffee bar at the Earl's Court end of the Old Brompton Road, and immediately I left school I went back there. The sound of the whirring coffee machines and the smell of brewing coffee beans blasted your senses the moment you opened the door. It was filled with interesting types, sitting at long wooden tables, reading John-Paul Sartre and the *Thoughts of Chairman Mao*. With candle wax pouring down the

161

sides of Chianti bottles and 'The Girl from Ipanema' and 'Desafinado' playing in the background, I could be making a cappuccino for Claudia Cardinale one minute and chatting to the regulars the next. When I first worked there, it was the age of Concrete Poetry, a concept my mother had made some attempt at explaining, although not very successfully. I think her appreciation of concrete didn't stretch much further than e.e. cummings.

That September I began at Queen's College in Harley Street, a course that included Business Studies ('Clare finds this subject quite beyond her'), housewifery and other subjects now forgotten and at which I was equally useless. I left after a year, and won't dwell on my achievements, or lack of them, but with a new batch of friends. Reading was still my passionate response to the world and it was at this time that I first read Antonia White's quartet of books beginning with *Frost in May*. Maeve had done the original dust jackets for *The Lost Traveller* and *The Sugar House* and I read all four books as if in a trance.

I walked around the house with a book in my hand, unable to bear interruption, transfixed by Clara Batchelor's convent childhood, her marriages, her affairs, her complex life and, finally, her terrible descent into madness. Everything was written with such power and lucidity, and I longed to meet Antonia White and tell her how I felt. Maeve arranged an introduction. She was kind, but seemed surprised by my reaction to her books. She thought me quite young to feel so deeply about books that had long been out of print, and described such a different time from my own. I thought her response odd. I couldn't understand her mystification at my loving what were obviously masterfully written books at any time. Perhaps she was puzzled because

I was so much a girl of my time, with the customary mini-skirt, long blonde hair and panda eyes, and probably looked as though all I did was flick through *Honey* magazine and re-apply my eyeliner. I asked questions about her books and she asked me questions about Mervyn, and we smiled shyly at each other as we talked. We drank our tea and ate the little jam sandwiches she had prepared in her flat in Gloucester Road and, as I got up to leave, she handed me a very battered copy of *Frost in May* that she inscribed for me: 'To Clare. With my best wishes and apologies for its being such a dirty copy & much appreciation for liking my other books! Antonia White'. Twenty years after Maeve died, and over thirty years after it was written, I came across this letter tucked inside her copy of *Frost in May*.

13 Ashburn Gardens, S.W.7.
20th June 1952

Dear Mrs Peake,

For over two years I have had a horribly guilty conscience. I've never thanked you personally for the beautiful jacket you did for The Lost Traveller. I remember how impressed I was at the wonderfully imaginative design you did for what seemed to me an impossible book to convey in a symbolic drawing as you did. Every time I look at it, I do so with fresh pleasure and everyone I know greatly admired it.

Now I have to thank you for the jacket for The Sugar House which I think is delightful. I am so glad you were able to do it as I particularly asked Eyre and Spottiswoode that you should. I hope to start a new

163

novel in the autumn and I shall certainly make the same request to the publishers when that is finished. If it ever is!

Thanking you again,

Yours sincerely,

Antonia White

Gloucester Road always had a quiet strength about it. It reminded me of an aged aunt – solid, reliable but never fashionable. It had a subdued authority, and I liked its completely unpretentious atmosphere. It was a criss-cross walk from my house to the station, but a far more interesting one than the direct walk along the Old Brompton Road to South Kensington, and there were always far more interesting diversions on the way. Quentin Crisp and I once had a memorably gentle stroll to the station after a lunch with Maeve. We chatted about everything, stopping to reply to a cockatoo who called to us from his cage set in the open window of a flat in Bina Gardens. I had friends at the Webber Douglas drama school in Clareville Street, and Elizabeth Taylor had set the beautiful and poignant Mrs Palfrey at the Clermont there.

It had also been the scene of some unpredictable acts of verbal and physical violence. I once deeply irritated an elderly woman, a complete stranger, who, on passing, suddenly turned and began screaming aggressively in my face, 'You bloody mermaids. I've had a bloody nuff of you bloody girls. Get your bloody hair cut, you bloody mermaid.' Her boredom with the army of hippies surrounding her wherever she turned had reached fever pitch and I must have been the straw that broke the camel's back. On another occasion, I had just bought a bag of overripe plums at the fruit stall outside the station when a swarthy man put his hand up my skirt and pinched my bottom. I was incredibly incensed by his nerve and, before I knew what I was doing, I was racing down the stairs after him, pelting him with my plums. I have an abiding image of this man pushing his way through the crowds as skin, stones and trickling juice slopped down his hair, neck and, as he turned to look at me, his extremely shocked face.

As with Antonia White, I felt similarly drawn to the photographs of Bill Brandt. I had bought myself *Shadow and Light*, a book I scrutinised endlessly until I knew the faces of his subjects almost as well as I knew my own. I found his number in the telephone directory and he invited me to his house to look at the originals. For an hour or so he led me round his cavernous flat, showing me one by one the images that I knew so well. Hung without so much as an inch between them were the miners, covered in soot and digging into their supper, the children playing in the war-torn East End streets, the ladies and gentlemen at Ascot, the portraits of distinguished British painters and writers. I asked him whether I could buy one, and we wandered around looking at the pictures again and again, until I finally decided on 'Wuthering Heights', which he took off his wall and I carried home.

Everything and everybody was accessible then. People didn't say no, or the people I wanted to meet didn't. Nobody was ex-directory, and people didn't seem to take themselves so seriously. I was used to it. Anyone who wanted to meet Mervyn just rung up and asked. After being told to 'piss off' under his breath when asking for the comedian and singer Dave King's autograph when I was six, I wasn't left with many illusions about showbiz types. Many of them seemed to do that peculiar thing of looking through you, or nervously meeting your eye, as though you were after a piece of their soul, something I had no interest at all in having. But there were always exceptions, real stars who didn't disappoint. Sebastian once spotted a hero of his walking along a street in Jersey. It was a moment unlikely to be repeated, so he buttonholed the fabulous Tommy Cooper, asked whether he could buy him a drink and then whiled away the next two hours in a deserted pub in St Helier, talking to that uniquely hilarious comedian.

First Job

I adored my mother's bedroom on the top floor of our house in Drayton Gardens. The candy-striped wallpaper had been hung in such a way that it felt as if you were under a big top at the circus, or an elegant marquee in the grounds of a grand house. The room was almost bare, and furnished only with a dressing-table (a ghastly, ultramodern piece she had bought with great extravagance from Peter Jones in the fifties), a brass bed, two rather beautiful chairs that had once belonged to her mother, Matty, and two huge paintings Sebastian had painted as a child. Her dressing-table housed her meagre collection of costume jewellery, and the gigantic amethyst bracelet Mervyn had bought her with the proceeds of his Society of Literature award for *Gormenghast* and volume of poetry, *The Glassblowers*. Each mirror in the three-sided dressing-table was about six inches wide and this was the only place in the house where you could study yourself, and then only in bits at a time. There were no full-length or even half-length mirrors in the house, not from any concern over pagan idolatry, but just because there weren't any. A small oval mirror above the sink in the minuscule bathroom and a broken shaving mirror in the kitchen put paid to any lurking vanity. But in Maeve's bedroom, I could look at myself in sections, by sitting, standing or crouching. Until I left home, I had never seen the whole of my body in one piece, unless I was in a shop or someone else's house, and then never naked.

Over the years, my tiny bedroom had gone through many transformations. It had been a Cornish fishing village, with shell-laden nets hanging from the ceiling and cockle-filled baskets sitting on the sand-painted floorboards; a French restaurant, with a small table covered with a blue and white checked tablecloth, candle-filled wine bottles and a huge string of onions that hung from the wall, bought from the French onion seller who cycled round our area once a fortnight. He wore the obligatory striped jumper and black beret and his neck was bent with the weight of so many onion necklaces. Finally, it was a reading room, with white walls and floorboards, and decorated with nothing other than the black, grey, green and orange of Penguin books to give it colour.

While my room was cluttered and disorganised, Maeve's was ordered and soothing. It was where I made my telephone calls, did my make-up, and got ready for the evening ahead. The room was light and had a feeling of absolute serenity, despite all the action happening on the street below. On her bedside table she kept a note-pad where she recorded everything she read, with a date, a short précis, and her thoughts on each book. She read all the time, was as lost without something 'on the go' as I was. If she was banned from reading, or went blind and couldn't master Braille, she would rather die she said. She had a few hypothetical situations she would rather die than face, all of them unlikely ever to happen. Bananas repelled her so utterly that you had merely to plant one near her nose (which I did once) for her to begin retching. Far worse than the smell of a banana was the thought that one day she might be forced to eat one. Peaches didn't fare much better. The furriness of the skin, the succulence of the flesh all anathema to her. Her major dread was being forced to spend even a second in a submarine. Apart from this, she was quite normal, unless of course it came to flat shoes.

Her cupboard stored her few but beautifully looked-after clothes. They were immensely glamorous, in whites and blacks and muddy greens and beiges. I can see her now, with her waist clinched tight in a Burberry raincoat, the collar turned up, the tight straight skirt underneath, the pencil thin stilettos, T-barred or ankle-strapped, the stork-like ankles always looking as though they might snap at any moment with the sheer weight of carrying a body around. The very word 'sensible' could lead her into a depression she said, so thought it much more sensible not to be sensible, and if your stilettos became uncomfortable and your feet ached, well that was just too bad.

My bedroom looked over the back garden, and the only sounds I heard were the warblings of jolly sparrows and the occasional mowing of the minuscule lawns of Chelsea. Maeve's faced the street and was a hotbed of sound and happening. An endless stream of cars and lorries rumbled along, using our street as a thoroughfare. The queue began forming at the Old Brompton Road, and then single-filed its way across the Fulham Road, King's Road and Cheyne Walk towards the river. The roar of London traffic and late-night partying could be heard distinctly, floating up the four floors, through her window and into her bedroom. I loved nothing more than being alone in the house, lying on her bed, listening to the traffic making its way around London and knowing that all I had to do was open my front door to be a part of it all.

The Drayton Arms was just across the road and every Sunday, if Fabian, by now married to Phyllida, and Sebastian, back from his travels, were at home, we all went there for a pre-lunch drink. We had been going there for years. It was a real neighbourhood pub, with a friendly proprietor, a roaring fire in the winter, and unchanging regulars, and there was something really pleasant about this weekly ritual. Another regular was Vyvyan Holland. I would glance at him, unable to comprehend that the man reading his paper, and enjoying a pint and a bag of cheese and onion crisps was Oscar Wilde's son. It seemed so extraordinary somehow. Since finding a miniature edition of *The Ballad of Reading Gaol* in my stocking one Christmas and reading *De Profundis* with a torch under my blankets at school, I had been fascinated. Oscar Wilde was from another time entirely, and had nothing whatsoever to do with the Drayton Arms. I always stopped myself from striking up a conversation; it would have been intrusive and insensitive to have interrupted his pre-lunch drink with some outpouring he had heard a million times before. But it didn't stop me looking and thinking about the history he must surely have anchored to his heart.

After our wines and beers and gin and tonics we would go home to the roast Maeve had been slow cooking for hours, sitting around the kitchen table in the basement, with just the family or with friends. At one of these lunches we became aware that we were being watched. On the window sill, observing us from the other side of the glass, was a large rat. Standing on his haunches he held half a cheese sandwich in his tiny human-like hands, and there was a look in his eye suggesting that he wanted to join in the fun. Although we should all have been shrieking by now, there was something rather touching about it, and we left him alone to enjoy his lunch.

Since I'd been such an unmitigated dunce at school, it was difficult to know quite what to do with me. It must have been a real source of curiosity for my mother, who was academically very able, but I just couldn't seem to do it. There was never so much as a hint of disappointment shown, although I'm sure that, over the years, occasional tosses and turns in the wee small hours must have produced one or two tangled sheets. I was never aware of it at the time and perhaps it never happened. Perhaps my mother would have said that not getting some good O-levels, although limiting for me, didn't worry her in the least. Had I shown no interest in the world about me, I'm sure it would have been a very different matter. Fabian had finished at Chelsea Art School and was now winning awards at the Royal College of Art, and Sebastian was a linguist and adventurer but, in my case, there didn't seem to be any recognisable talent for anything. Outsiders' expectations were more difficult. Would I paint, would I write, would I create? they seemed to be saying. No, was the very bald answer.

On my first day at speedwriting, before I'd even hung up my coat, I was led into the ladies by a phenomenally pretty girl I'd never set eyes on before. 'Shall we have a smoke before we begin?' Sarah said. Holding my hand she took me into a tiny cubicle where we shared a joint and introduced ourselves. Maeve, quietly despairing, had seen an advertisement on the tube. 'Gt a gd jb' it said. It was an eight-week secretarial course where you repeated the weeks until you had mastered speedwriting. I left after nine months, still on week one, but it was there I met the girls who would turn out to be friends I kept for life.

Speedwriting was located above Freeman, Hardy and Willis in Oxford Street. As well as selling shoes, the shop had a children's clothes department, and in the clothes department was a cafe. After the stifledom of school, I was invigorated to meet girls with the same passions as I had for the cinema, the theatre, books and music, and it made it virtually impossible ever to leave that coffee bar. Speedwriting was crammed with girls who looked as though they had answered an advertisement touting for the physically blessed. I had never before seen so many beautiful, captivating, sexy, naughty, intelligent girls in one small space. Aside from my new friend, Sarah Coats, a jaw-droppingly lovely, aristocratic, small girl, none of the other girls appeared to have smoked on their homework breaks. They were all built like racehorses, with endless tawny limbs, flawless skin and cheekbones so sculpted that, for the first time in my life, I felt, at a perfectly average five foot four, like a chirpy midget. There were Russian princesses and granddaughters of Churchill, the achingly hip and the fantastically rich, sitting side by side, headphones on, hoping to find what it took to gt a gd jb.

Zoë Wanamaker, a big-hearted, witty and incredibly stylish girl, took me to weekly work-out classes with Lotte Berk, to Praed Street to obtain morning-after pills and, in a rare moment when we weren't laughing, made a sterling attempt to clarify the Six-day War to me. In Sue, I found a glamorous and earthy friend with the same love of the cinema as I had. After a monstrously boring day speed-writing, we would saunter to the Curzon, or the Odeon Leicester Square, or hop on a tube to the National Film Theatre, to look at old and new films. Minus the nerd factor, Sue was fantastically knowledgeable, a real movie buff, and we never tired of talking, over endless cups of black coffee, of the glory of Catherine Deneuve and her equally attractive sister, Françoise Dorleac, on whom we both had crushes. We watched *Belle du Jour*, *Les Parapluies de Cherbourg* and *Cul de Sac* over and over again, and the unrelated *A Man and a Woman*. The slim plotline didn't worry us in the least, and had us dreaming of kissing men in the teeming rain with Da da da da da, dardardar, da da da da da, dardardar da da da da da dardardar daar daar, dar dar da dar da playing in the background.

My other great friend was Georgie, a giant in every sense of the word. She and her long-legged mother, Kate, lived in a doll's house in Rutland Street, Knightsbridge. Kate and I had the same birthday, a fact she never remembered. 'No darling, we haven't, have we? Are you serious? We've got the same birthday, how extraordinary, no wonder I love you,' she said for the next twenty-five years. Georgie was the first truly sophisticated young person I'd ever come across. Her boyfriends were urbane London men who bought her expensive jewellery and took her for dinner, or cockney wide boys who made her laugh and took her to the dogs. One night she might be going out with Mr Chow, the next John Binden. In the evenings, she worked as a waitress in Gasworks restaurant and, like Zoë and Sue, also wanted to be an actress.

Thinking me an innocent, Kate had nuggets of wisdom

prepared for any occasion. Delivered with great authority, these sage words were whispered deep and low, as though she were letting me in on the secret of life itself. 'Men love girls with sticky out teeth. It's very sexy, you see, Clare.' 'Never trust a small woman. They are tough and manipulative.' 'Never, but never, have a plain girlfriend. They'll take your man. Men love plain women.' 'Die rather than show your arms past thirty.' 'Never show a man you're keen; he'll go off you.' And most bewildering of all, 'Paul McCartney only likes girls with fat legs and no bosom.'

I laughed a lot and was startled by Kate's 'all men are bastards' dictum every other sentence. This theory was a new one to me. But the 'treat 'em mean and keep 'em keen' philosophy could have been invented by Kate herself, as she did treat them mean and she did keep them keen. At fifty-seven, there were men of all ages happy to be treated by Kate in any way at all, as long as they were treated. She was spectacularly elegant, utterly unafraid, horrible to men, sympathetic to women, incredibly attractive to both sexes, and absolutely mad about her daughter. She took enormous delight in shocking Georgie and me with her Homerically epic tales of deceit, rivalry and adventure in the thirties, and, while I found her stories wonderfully risqué and hysterically funny, Georgie could be quite thrown by them. Between them, her parents had been married five times and at seventeen Georgie was like a very pretty girl of twenty-five or thirty. They were a glamorous duo and I was entranced.

Every day after college, Georgie came to my house or I went to hers, and after she had hoovered, dusted, arranged flowers, prepared a light supper for Kate, polished some brass and written her thank-you letters, we were ready to begin the preparations for the night. Entirely due to

Georgie's influence, I took more than my customary five minutes to get ready. Georgie took hours, not that our clothes took long to assemble. Our skirts, like everybody else's, were the width of a belt, our skinny ribs were bought two sizes smaller than we took, and our shoes were sling-backed and stilettoed. It was the make-up that took the time. There were the pale brown freckles to dot on our noses, the liquid eyeliner to coat our eyelids, the false eyelashes to glue to the top, the eyelashes to paint on the bottom, the baby pink blusher to rouge our cheeks, the pan stick to obliterate our mouths and the Je Reviens to squirt. Then we were ready.

There was absolutely no chance of either of us falling in love with one another's boyfriends because the type I liked didn't fall into either of her categories. I liked pretty boys who looked ill and sensitive, with no bottoms and sunken cheeks – the cool thin boy slumped in a corner, the boy who walked everywhere, had no money, and hung around Parson's ignoring you after he had kissed you all night at a party the night before. Georgie liked sophisticated men at both ends of the social strata, men who knew what was what.

But for all her maturity, Georgie could be unpredictable. One filthy night we went to the flat of a group of boys we knew and they offered us some LSD. Neither of us had taken a trip before, and there was no doubt that Georgie would refuse, I could have bet my life on it. 'No thanks' and 'Yes please' came out of our mouths simultaneously, but out of the wrong mouths. I was staggered but thought if the responsible Georgie can, I can. We were given our little pieces of blotting paper and hung around waiting for our journey to begin. It seemed to be having no effect so, feeling

175

extremely relieved, we decided to make our way back home. We glided out of the flat in West Kensington to be pistol whipped by the spiteful rain lashing at us horizontally. 'Don't look, walk straight on as if you haven't noticed,' Georgie bossed. 'Haven't noticed what?' I asked. 'Our knickers,' she screamed. 'Look, they're down by our ankles.' We shuffled along the Cromwell Road for the next mile or so like two geisha girls with newly bound feet, our twin knickers wrapped around our ankles.

It seems odd that I could be so influenced by her trip that I believed my knickers had also fallen down. We hailed an aeroplane that had fortuitously stopped on the runway where we were standing and, although it took days to reach my house, the pilot didn't seem to find anything peculiar about us. I left Georgie to continue her journey, and went into what I thought would be the safety of my home. I undressed and lay in bed and, for what seemed like minutes, but turned out to be five or six hours, I watched in awe and respectful silence as the hands on my clock transformed themselves into a glamorous and heavily made up Margot Fonteyn and Rudolph Nureyev. Their dancing was sublime and inexhaustible and it was only when they left my clock to clamber up my curtains for an encore that I became frightened. I crept into my mother's bedroom on my hands and knees, got into her bed, woke her up, terrified her with my ramblings and eventually fell asleep.

A few hours later I tried to reach Georgie, but her mother Kate said she was in a mysteriously deep slumber. Georgie rang me the following morning. She had been up all night, she said, looking at herself in the mirror, and was so staggered by her beauty that she couldn't stop admiring herself for a single second. When she eventually forced her

176

eyes off herself for a brief moment, then returned to gaze at her visage, the image that greeted her was that of Cliff Richard. All through the night, she discovered she could change her face at will, until she had first-hand knowledge of what it felt like to be Julie Christie, Serge Gainsbourg, Sidney Poitier and Rita Tushingham. Although I was only an observer, I also felt I now had intimate knowledge of what trials and tribulations a ballerina goes through. I had seen for myself the bloody feet.

Although my figure wasn't fashionable, at least I had the advantage of never having to iron my hair, as most of my friends did. One afternoon I was approached by a man in the Old Brompton Road, asking me to join him for a coffee as he had a proposition to make. Although middle-aged, he didn't seem particularly threatening, and I was curious. Over coffee, he told me that he had a magazine called *Penthouse*, which had tastefully done nude and semi-nude photographs. Would I be interested in being in it? He felt I had a future career in glamour modelling. I said I'd let him know, kept his card in my wallet for a few years, but never rang. Although I felt vaguely flattered, a glamour model was something I had no desire to be, and if that was the impression I was giving to complete strangers, then I had to do something about it. I rushed to the chemist, bought some gauze and attempted tourniqueting my bosom into a squashed macaroon so as to camouflage the bloody thing. Flat chests were de rigueur; no one wanted a cleavage. Outwardly, the boys solemnly confessed they couldn't agree more, although privately, I couldn't help but notice, it seemed to be a slightly different matter.

I had done all these courses, but none was going to secure me the job of a secretary, a business woman or even a

177

housewife, so I was nervously looking forward to beginning work for my mother's great friend Hazel as her maid. I hadn't the first idea of what being a maid involved, but it sounded fun and, on that first morning, we decided between us what the term meant. Hazel lived in a gigantic flat off Victoria Street and I began working for her when I was seventeen. Sebastian had preceded me when he'd been employed as a kind of un-uniformed valet. She loved the theatre but always became uncomfortable during a performance due to a botched suicide attempt some years earlier. Eventually she found the solution. She bought a vast and cumbersome blow-up cushion, not dissimilar in appearance to a whoopee cushion, which Sebastian carried in front of him like one of three kings bearing a gift. She then made herself comfortable and the people behind her infuriated.

He also ran some of her errands, but I soon found out for myself that these excursions were never as simple as the scrawled list implied. On closer inspection, her lists were daunting and unconventional to say the least. One carrot, seven screwdrivers, an Alice band, a plank of cedarwood and some Michaelmas daisies were the kind of thing she might be after. It was like a living, breathing game of 'I went to Paris to buy . . .'. 'Is that enough, Sebastian?' Hazel would drawl as she handed him twenty-five crisp pound notes.

An Alice band in Victoria Street may not have been the hardest thing in the world to find, but the more obscure the demand, the more frustrated Sebastian became. So, for some extraordinary reason, it was suggested that I take over where he left off, and so began my first proper paid job. Hazel was a Guggenheim, the sister of Peggy and the daughter of the millionaire who famously changed into his dinner jacket in preparation for his plunge into that black ocean from the sinking *Titanic*. Hazel was immensely rich, and surrounded by hangers-on and opportunists, a breed I had never come across before. I was shocked by these people and found their lack of respect for Hazel revolting. I arrived early every morning to identify the clothes she wanted to wear for the day, but it could be tricky as Hazel didn't appreciate being a size or four larger than she had once been, and preferred to wear her clothes a few sizes smaller. Together we improvised. Her yellow hair hung down in natural ringlets and, although at least sixty-five, she still had the most lovely face, with pale unlined skin and a flawless complexion.

On her mantelpiece sat a photograph taken on her eighteenth birthday. She had been exquisitely pretty and reminded me of a girl in an F. Scott Fitzgerald book, or a southern belle from a Tennessee Williams play, and she always appeared to me utterly out of place in London. They said that Peggy had been born with the brains and Hazel with the beauty and, as I gazed at the photograph every day while dusting, I imagined Hazel's life as the adored daughter of one of the richest men in America; and whenever I heard the Noël Coward song 'Poor Little Rich Girl', I thought of Hazel. She could be a nightmare to work for, neurotic and pernickety, but she was always kind and I knew she liked me as I liked her.

But then I always adored older women. Even though I knew that Jean Shrimpton and Twiggy looked great, it was Jeanne Moreau, Simone Signoret and Sophia Loren who captivated me – anyone, in fact, full featured, sensual and bruised, who seemed to have lived, loved and ached. I just loved that intelligent, head held high, flawed kind of woman. I never became one. Like Hazel, I was far too fond of frills and fluff, and much too polite to be mysterious.

We were forever at cross-purposes. Her requests were invariably abstract, so when, one day, she said, ' Draw me a bath, Clarabelle,' I didn't question it, and she didn't question my request for a piece of paper and a pencil. Since I was so hopeless at drawing, it was a moment or two before either of us realised my mistake. We went along in this curious and hypothetical way for a year or so, and it suited us both very well.

One day she decided it was time she held a party. When the big day arrived, I busied myself with the stream of delivery men, carting in vast supplies of food, boxes of champagne, crates of wine, patisseries from Gloriette and exotic flowers from Moyses Stevens. Along with assorted butlers and maids, I listened as Hazel issued her peculiar requests from her bedroom and we jumped to it. 'I'm gonna stay in bed for the party, Clarabelle, so I want you to fix the back of my dress.' There *was* no back of the dress. She had just managed to squeeze the front over her head, and somehow fit her arms through the tiny puff sleeves but, for the width of a foot or so, her back was uncovered. So that the dress didn't gape, I had to work out a way of joining the back together. Someone was sent out for strips of pink elastic and I sewed them so that the dress met at last. She stayed in it as I sewed, and we both felt extremely proud of ourselves when, from the front, it looked like a perfectly fitting outfit.

Hazel was newly in love, so she was deliriously happy that night. Her suitor was a handsome South American, about thirty years her junior, whose motives were obvious to everyone but her. She must have known, but then she had never expected anyone to be interested in her for anything *but* her money. I hated him on sight, and tried to make it

180

clear by a lot of subtle eyebrow lifting and almost imperceptible nodding of my head that I was on to him (as if he'd care). The party was a success. While Norman Mailer paced the flat, leering at my sister-in-law, Phyllida, I watched old smarmy, Hazel's beau, as he faked desire and Hazel disingenuously fell for it. But anyway, her sweet heart was broken soon after, not for the first time I'm sure, but perhaps for the last. I was far too young, too inexperienced and too fond of Hazel to have been any help, but I did notice, and I did hurt for her. She went to live in New Orleans soon after, returning to the southern gal she had always been. I never saw her again, but I never forgot.

Years later a friend bought me a biography of the Guggenheim family, a curious present in all kinds of ways but particularly since I had never mentioned Hazel to her. I went straight to the index and found the chapter on my friend. It was a terrible shock to read of the horrific deaths of her two baby sons, who'd fallen from the balcony of her Manhattan apartment when she'd been a young woman. She was with them when they fell, and although it isn't clear what happened on that terrible day, I had known nothing of the tragedy that coloured Hazel's life, and if my mother knew, she never told me.

La Vie en Rose

O ver the years I lived in Drayton Gardens, there had been many boyfriends, and the kitchen was the scene for many break-ups and make-ups. A lot of listening to 'Otis Blue' and weeping into glasses of gin went on there, but I loved that place, with the scrubbed wooden table that smelt of bleach. The wood had almost forgotten what tree it had come from after decades of manic scrubbing, with undiluted bleach poured on to it every day, until all you had to do was put a paper napkin on to its proud and pale surface and it left a mark. Everything worth happening happened there, and I have more nostalgia for that warm room in the basement than I have for anywhere else in the world.

The whole room was muralled. Dad had begun when we first moved in, painting strange little faces peering from holes in the wall where plaster had crumbled off and not been filled, then Mum took over and couldn't stop. Our shutters, boiler, oven, dresser, walls, cupboards and fridge were all painted. The staircase to the kitchen had a wooden handrail and on the wall behind it Maeve had painted dancers, men and women dressed in leotards and tutus with their feet resting on the rail as if in a dance studio. There was a Welsh dresser with un-matching but lovely china, and an airing cupboard that smelt of newly laundered sheets, warmth and excitement. Our presents, bought months before Christmas and birthdays, would be hidden among the tablecloths, towels and sharply creased napkins, and I don't think she ever knew I had discovered this hiding place years before. Baby Bunting, our white cat, coiled on top of the towels, purring contentedly, full from the prawns and occasional potted shrimps – or shrotted pimps, as Maeve called them – she ate with her paw, and double cream she lapped with her tongue. Slim, healthy and spoilt, she was confident in the knowledge that she was queen of the castle and would never be disturbed.

There was no washing machine, spin dryer or any modern convenience at all, except for a small wooden clothes-line that went up in the morning and came down in the evening. I remember the thud of the pastry as it hit the floured kitchen table, the rolling that went on until it was light enough to cover the apple pie or steak and kidney pie or the criss-cross of the treacle tart Maeve would be preparing for supper. She was very proud of the lightness of her pastry, saying that, like everything else in life, you either had it or you didn't. I remember the beauty of the coalmen as they delivered the coal to our bunker, just outside the kitchen door. Why, Maeve pondered, were coalmen and firemen *always* handsome? Was it a necessity when applying for the job?

Before going out at night I would run the four floors to the basement, a quick blast of 'Pet Sounds' or 'Tapestry' on the record player, do my make-up in the minute mirror perched on a tiny ledge on the dresser, and leave the house to walk to the Royal Court to see all the new plays in the opening week. I miss those days. I miss those nights when I would come home to find Maeve in the kitchen, talking and drinking with her friends. It might be John Davenport, the literary critic who, when temporarily homeless, stayed with us and who, in the middle of the night, I once saw standing naked in the lavatory, waving cheerily as I passed him by and taking what looked like rather an unsteady aim. It might be John Braine, author of *Room at the Top*, with his sexy northern accent – 'Ooh Maeve! Just what the doctor ordered,' he'd say as he tucked into apple crumble – or Gordian Gill, Eric Gill's adopted son, a sweet and touching man for whom nothing ever seemed to go right. There could be laughter with Michael Moorcock while they ate his favourite meal of roast lamb followed by chocolate mousse. Sometimes it would be a Scrabble contest with Brigid Brophy, a philosophical discussion with Lord Longford, or a melancholy talk with the gentle Arabella Boxer, or nostalgic reminiscences with Quentin Crisp or new ideas with Michael Horowitz, Heathcote Williams and other young poets who had become friends.

I might come home to find her sitting with Tony, our window-cleaner. On a few occasions she had found him looking at the books in the sitting room, and hastily putting them back on the shelves. One morning they got talking about their favourite authors and, from then on, once a month after cleaning the windows, he gave himself an extra hour to sit and have coffee with Maeve and talk about the book he was reading. He 'wasn't allowed' to buy books (dust harbourers) or borrow books from the library, because his wife was intimidated by his 'hobby' and became incensed when he wanted to read in silence instead of watching television with her. So he secreted them under the cloths in his van, found a place to park and read in his lunch breaks.

I was livid when I heard this story. I couldn't believe he was being prevented from doing what he loved by his wife and, at the time, didn't understand, or didn't want to understand, the loneliness both he and his wife must have been feeling. This book group of two temporarily solved the problem.

It is impossible to listen to 'La Vie en Rose' without conjuring up the whole of my childhood. That gorgeous space in the basement, with Edith Piaf belting out the chirpier 'Mon Manège à Moi', my mother circling the room with the vegetable she was peeling gripped in her hand, the two of us passionately joining in every word, one of us understanding what they were singing, the other without a clue. Or stopping whatever we were doing – cooking, cleaning, washing up – and dancing together to Ella Fitzgerald's 'Misty' or Billie Holiday's 'Night and Day' and 'The Man I Love', tears welling up in our eyes, hearts bursting with gorgeously indulgent emotion, loving every second of that most satisfying of small pleasures.

Maeve held a big party about twice a year. The kitchen would be waiting patiently in the basement, spruced and smart, smelling glorious and just hanging around until the guests made the exodus from the elegant sitting room two floors up. She never felt that parties were for serious conversation; you had the rest of your life for that. They were for letting your hair down, for dancing and disgracing yourself, for forgetting your troubles and having some fun. She would retrieve her cane and her collapsible top hat from the airing cupboard and dance as if her life depended on it, as of course it did. The party often ended with Maeve standing on the kitchen table, her top hat perched sideways, her magician's cane elongated for her Marlene Dietrich impression. 'Falling in love again, never wanted to, what am I to do, I can't heeeelp it,' she would imitate brilliantly with all the seduction of Lili Marlene, halfway there already with her enormous eyelids, and infuriatingly perfect show-girl legs.

I can see Maeve and Michael Moorcock now, he in an elegant Harris Tweed suit, she with a white feather boa casually slung around her neck, swaying, tango-ing, laughing. The parties, heaving with poets and publishers, translators and editors, writers and painters ended with the same song for years. 'All You Need is Love' would belt out from the ancient record player, and she would sing along, vehemently endorsing the message. I should have been embarrassed, but I never was. I was proud. I never wanted one of those comfortable mothers who didn't take life by the throat and squeeze it. I liked her daring. I liked it that when her heart was breaking, she rose to the occasion. And I couldn't stand some of the crusty academics who stood in a corner, observing and drinking, drinking and observing, the voyeurs who would have died rather than let themselves go, but never in a million years would have refused an invitation, because no one gave a party like Maeve.

Years after she died, I realised that she had never taught me anything practical at all, apart from a few little culinary tips. 'A bit of ash in the stew makes all the difference, darling,' she laughingly said as I watched her stirring the deliciously warming stew with ash precariously bent from her cigarette. She was a hopeless smoker. She didn't inhale and always looked as if she was trying out her first cigarette, as she puffed awkwardly, if she puffed at all. She soon graduated to cigars, and they suited her much better. A really good cigar gave her as much pleasure, if not more, than a tipple of Gordon's or a bottle of Arpège. But this lack of any education whatsoever in the field of house-proudness made the concept fraught with misunderstanding, and like another language to me. When I met Charlie, the man I was going to marry, I entered another world, with people who, it seemed, spoke in tongues. 'When did you last wash your wainscotting, Clare?' my mother-in-law once asked me in a voice laden with accusation. I was too scared to admit that I hadn't a clue what she was talking about, but felt sure it must be a secret part of my anatomy. There were hundreds of these words, and when I asked Maeve what they meant, she didn't know either.

But she knew what a party was for and I was very happy with a mother who laughed and danced and drank too much on occasions. Having said that, after I had meticulously learnt Zorba's Dance at twilight on a beach in Athens a few years later, I unwisely taught it to Maeve. We happily practised on impromptu occasions when we were alone, but soon it became another regular finale to her parties when she gave me the eye that signalled a rather shameful *pas de deux*, outstretched arms and often unsynchronised foot movements stamping to the strains of Theodorakis's mandolins.

Maeve was a complex woman, and there were many contradictions. Aside from being glamorous and vivacious, she was intensely private. She appeared cool and supremely confident, but underneath it all she was nervy and extremely shy. She was a serious person and the idea of discussing her personal life with anyone who wasn't the greatest of friends would repulse her in the same way it repulses me. She would have got on badly in this world where nothing is private, and everyone kisses each other. Hating over-familiarity, her composure could be stiff with strangers, yet with close friends and family she was warm and earthy. She loved her two best friends, Barbara Norman and Sue French,

187

deeply, but whether she talked to them about the inner workings of her soul I'll never know. She claimed to loathe sentimentality, hated to be manipulated, was furious with herself for crying so uncontrollably at the death of Bambi's mother, and found babies, even her own, a bit of a bore. Yet didn't I catch her on a few occasions choking up when she saw big men holding tiny babies, or lovers unaware they were being observed? The truth is, while Sebastian and Fabian don't have a trickle of sentimentality coursing through their veins, Mervyn, Maeve and I were emotional beings, who could sob at the breaking of a stalk and thoroughly enjoy every moment.

Walking with Purpose in New York

In September 1968, Maeve and I went to New York. Mervyn's books were to be re-published in America; Maeve had been invited for the launch and thought it would be fun if I went with her. Although I knew I would miss my new boyfriend, Gerry, and worry about what he was up to, I wasn't going to miss a chance like this. I had been on a plane once before, an ill-fated school trip to Rome for an audience with the Pope. It wasn't the intimate tête-à-tête with His Holiness I had envisioned, but a squashed few hours among the teeming throngs of worldwide Roman Catholics in St Peter's Square, and a huge disappointment.

Apart from the Witterings, I'd rarely left London, so a trip to New York was far more of an experience than it sounds. We bade farewell to Sebastian at Gloucester Road Air Terminal, all of us nervy and two of us already homesick. It was a dreadful flight. I had never registered the word turbulent before, but the meaning soon became clear as we began to dip and rise and rock from side to side with a terrifying rhythm. Maeve and I searched each other's dilated pupils and nodded our wordless goodbyes as, clasping hands, we prayed to Jesus. I imagined myself digging maggots from my legs with a stick I'd carved in the jungle, and eating grasshoppers to survive when we eventually crashed. I'd been struck by a documentary I'd recently seen on the aftermath of a plane crash, and had been particularly impressed by the story of a girl who existed on insects and grubs, brushing up on her flora and fauna as she awaited rescue. There would be a documentary about me soon. Geographic accuracy had never been a strong point.

I had once witnessed my mother's apoplectic fury at her sister Matty's tactless remark, 'Do you think Clare might be a little short on the grey matter?' as I excitedly pointed out St Paul's Cathedral while driving through a side street in Barnes. So it didn't occur to me that there might not have been a jungle to crash into when we eventually went down, or that drowning was a more probable ending to my life. At that point, particulars were immaterial.

Eventually, our flight settled down and we arrived safely. When, with a dreadful shock, I noticed the thickness of my ankles, I almost wished we hadn't. Too excitable for jet lag, I left the Gramercy Park Hotel early the next morning to go record-shopping for my boyfriend. Stepping on to the pavement, I was immediately pinned against the hotel wall by a massive man wielding a knife and demanding my money. Mugging was in its infancy, the craze had yet to be imported, so I didn't know anyone in London who had experienced it. It was all over in a flash. He was charming, thanked me profusely, and promised to be back at the same time the next day to repay the debt. Thanking him, I went back up to my room, collected more money and headed out to find the records on my list, the as yet unreleased in England 'Mixed Bag' by Richie Havens,

'Lenny Bruce Live' and 'Music From Big Pink' by The Band.

Ballantine Books were publishing the *Titus* books and John and Betty Ballantine generously and imaginatively planned our trip to include as many aspects of American life as they were able to in the time we had. We met a gourmet, another word new to me. Never having taken food particularly seriously, and having taken good, home-cooked food for granted, it seemed such a very funny occupation, or preoccupation, to have. Undeterred by my complete lack of interest, he took us on outings to the best restaurants in town. I tasted lasagne for the first time in Little Italy, and ate my first Chinese food in Chinatown, where course after course had my taste buds screaming with gratitude. When our plump gentleman friend wasn't sampling European, Mediterranean or Asiatic grub, he could be found in the discos of New York, strutting his stuff and shaking his tail feather. He asked me if I'd like to go to a disco with him and, if so, to dress 'UP UP UP'. I can't remember exactly what I wore, but it would have been a variation on a theme: a 1930s lace dress from the Chelsea Antique Market, a sequinned cardigan, a floppy hat of some description, a pair of custom-made silver boots by Annello and Davide, and a fitted 1940s crepe or tweed jacket. I didn't have many clothes, but I adored the ones I had. I wouldn't have been caught dead in anything new and only bought 'old' clothes and the occasional treat from Quorum or Foale and Tuffin, so I'm sure I was a bit of a disappointment. I was neither elegant nor mini-skirted, and if anybody bothered to look I imagine we made a rather incongruous couple.

He dressed perfectly normally if, for my tastes, rather conservatively, on our gourmet outings (I was used to boys

191

in velvet suits, frilly shirts and fedora hats), but to my horror he arrived in a baby-blue satin, all-in-one disco outfit, zipping from his crotch to his neck in a meandering snake. A matching belt strained at the waist and sparkly jewels covered his ankles, and the whole ensemble was such a snug fit it left nothing to the imagination. A bejewelled headband carefully placed around his short, side-parted hair sat as proud as the jumpsuit, and his bespectacled face sported the same gung-ho enthusiasm minus smiles as when clad in a three-piece suit. As we walked down Lexington Avenue in search of a cab, his plump bottom wiggled with confidence, and I wanted to run back to the hotel and die of shame. He led me into the disco, a vast area with strobe lights and smoke pelting from an incinerator, and we temporarily forgot our disappointment in each other as we danced to the wonderfully danceable music, my new friend swirling and twirling like there was no tomorrow, arms flailing, feet scuttling in a trance of disco delight. I adored the music and valiantly tried to keep up but, being more hippy than disco girl, I had none of the moves. It had been a great night but when I next saw him it was as though it had never been. He was back in the land of bespoke tailors and serious con- noisseurs of the taste buds, and disco madness was just a faint memory until next Friday.

Maeve must have been meeting publishers because I did a lot of walking around New York alone, and I loved it. I found Brentano's bookshop and treated myself to American editions of my favourite writer at the time, Thomas Wolfe. I bought *Look Homeward Angel*, *You Can't Go Home Again* and *The Web and the Rock*. I bought *Down These Mean Streets a Man Must Go*, a book of literary criticism on Raymond Chandler. I bought *Lenny Bruce Uncut*, Djuna Barnes's

Nightwood and Bob Dylan's *Don't Look Back*. I bought beautiful editions of Robert Frost and Wallace Stevens poetry, Baudelaire's *Fleur du Mal*, and Enid Starkey's biography of Rimbaud, and I was in heaven. There was something about the jackets that intoxicated me and, like other people's make-up, these editions seemed imbued with something more wonderful than I could get at home. There were sofas in the bookshop and I found myself at closing time still sitting, surrounded by more books I wanted to take home but couldn't, due to lack of money and suitcase space. I walked out of the bookshop into the sunlight and I saw no ambling; everybody walked with purpose, so I walked with purpose, too.

I was invited to a party, and again I went alone. Arriving at the downtown loft, I was greeted by a group of strangers, beaming at me and welcoming me as though we were old friends. I was astonished to be told the party was being held in my honour, as Mervyn's daughter, astonished by the generosity of the Americans in going to the trouble of throwing a party for the daughter of a writer they'd never met. In one corner sat a naked woman, a cello between her legs, her wild Janis Joplin hair covering then uncovering her ample bosom, heaving away to a less than spellbound audience. She was ignored as I was encircled by twenty Carry On aficionados urging me to 'talk in your talk', prodding and cuddling me as if I were an alien recently disembarked from a spaceship. Joints the size of matchsticks were passed around with tweezers as I told them all I knew of Barbara Windsor and Kenneth Connor, searching frantically for anecdotal references to the Carry On team tucked somewhere deep in my subconscious.

We packed in a lot, my mother and I. One day we sat in

a deserted cinema in Times Square and watched an early morning showing of a new film, *The Graduate*, a toe-curlingly awful matinee of *A Midsummer Night's Dream*, took a disrespectfully brief look at the Klees in the Guggenheim, and went on an outing to a new play off, off, off Broadway, all in one twelve-hour stint. We'd been given some advice by the people taking us to the off-Broadway theatre. It was in a 'particularly rough neighbourhood', imperative that we dress down, that we didn't draw attention to ourselves – water off a duck's back for me, but trickier for my mother, who could dress in a paper bag and make it look couture. 'Avoid eye contact, keep your head down, ignore everyone, and keep walking,' was the advice given by these native New Yorkers. Nervously, we followed it to the letter and it wouldn't go down as one of the more pleasant journeys of my life. After politely stepping over bums and junkies lying abandoned on the pavements, I was shocked by the desolation, and saddened by how invisible these people seemed to be.

Nothing happened and, after a tense and miserable journey, we were very fed up to be informed that there were rules to seeing this play. Banned from sitting with the people we had come with, I was at first put out, but ten minutes later thanking the Lord I was sitting next to strangers. The entire male cast was naked. It wasn't the nakedness per se that embarrassed me; it was the intense physicality of this performance in the round. In such a small space, all the action was happening about a foot from my face. I longed to have a friend with me. I wanted to be able to giggle at the shrivelled willies and harmoniously swaying balls of the solemn actors, and it was catching a glimpse of my mother on the other side of the tiny theatre that had my nostrils flaring and my shoulders heaving with pent-up hysteria.

Our final weekend was spent with the Ballantines at their house in Bearsville, Woodstock, in the West Saugerty mountains. We got a cab from our hotel to Grand Central Station and, naturally, I thought of Elizabeth Smart as we sat and waited for our train.

I hadn't realised just how thrilling a railway station could be. I half expected a musical number to begin; the hustle and bustle was so exaggerated it seemed almost self-conscious, a show put on for visitors, and I wouldn't have been surprised to see one of Cyd Charisse's lovely legs popping out from behind some puffing steam as the whistle went. All I remember of the train journey was a guard who kept pestering a little black boy who was helping a woman clean the compartments. 'You OK, Choc-drop? Hey, Choccy, you OK?' The little boy didn't answer.

The Ballantines' house was in a magnificent part of the country. The redwood trees were as tall as the sky and the streams, painted wooden houses and log cabins were to my untravelled eye too glorious for words. By a quirk of fate, the house next to the Ballantines *was* The Big Pink. Not yet having heard the record I had just bought for my boyfriend, I was yet to fall in love with Rick Danko, my eventual dream man, or fully appreciate my close proximity to those beautiful and inspirational musicians. I could have knocked on the door and introduced myself. I could have struck up a conversation with Bob Dylan's children playing in the garden next door. I like to think I might have stood as much of a chance as anyone else of becoming Mrs Danko or the second Mrs Dylan. I could dream, I just couldn't knock.

195

Arriving home I found my boyfriend had been very well looked after by a girlfriend of ours and, in answer to my heartbroken 'whys', was informed with two pairs of steady arms around my shoulders, 'Oh Clare, we missed you so.' Perplexed, I let it go.

Meeting Titus Groan

I hadn't read the *Titus* books. There had never been any pressure to do so, and I was biding my time until the moment felt right, but they were always there at my shoulder, awaiting my response, and I knew that I couldn't put it off much longer. I don't know what I was frightened of, maybe the closeness, maybe that I wouldn't like them. My opinion wouldn't matter to my father, who had long since forgotten he had ever written them, but my opinion mattered to me.

Since the reissue of the trilogy by Penguin Modern Classics, the books had reached cult status. Everywhere I looked people were reading them, discussing them; every tube and every bus I travelled on seemed to have one person with an open copy of *Titus Groan* or *Gormenghast* in their hands. I was always on edge, terrified of comments that might upset me. Sitting at a kitchen table at a heaving party, I overheard a boy discussing my father. 'Oh, he's mad you know, he's in a bin,' he said. I searched for my boyfriend among the crowds. 'Please take me home,' I begged, as I registered the sneer I felt powerless to do anything about.

I finished *The Heart is a Lonely Hunter* and picked up *Titus Groan* and I loved it from the very first sentence. The words jumped from the pages and sucked me headlong into the corridors, the library, the kitchens, the attic. Oh Daddy! Why couldn't I tell you how proud I was?

Although Fuchsia, the fifteen-year-old heroine of the story, was based on Maeve as a girl, what subsequently happens to her when her father loses his mind was happening to me. When I read Fuchsia's reverie, published five years before I was born, it was as though my father had written it with me in mind, some self-fulfilling prophecy.

O dear father let me comfort you and you must never be like that again never never never and I will be your sentry for always always your sentry and will never talk to other people never only you my dear pale man and none will come near you only perhaps the doctor when you want him but only when you do and I will bring you flowers of every kind of colour and shape and speckled stones that look like frogs and ferns and all the beautiful things I can find and I will find books for you and will read to you all day and all night and never let you know that I'm tired and we shall go for walks when you are better and you will become happy happy if only you could be if only sad thin broken face so pale and none else would be there not my mother nor anyone nor Steerpike no no not him, he is too hard and clever not like you who are more clever but with kindness and not quick with clever words. I can see his mouth his mouth oh Dr Prune quick quick the blackness and he's going far away and the voice Dr Prune quick the voice is

going far away of Barquentine is going far away I cannot
see no no oh black my Dr Prune the black is swaying
swaying

I finished *Titus Groan* and began *Gormenghast*. I finished
Gormenghast and began *Titus Alone*, the final book. I knew
how difficult it had been to write. It had to be painstakingly
transcribed by Langdon Jones, a patient, gentle man, from
almost indecipherable exercise books and note-pads. I knew
that people were disappointed with the last book, but they
couldn't possibly know it had been written in confusion and
despair, and that to write a shopping list, let alone a book,
was a miracle. I picked up the books of poetry, I read
everything I could, and I began to get an idea of my father.
It had been impossible to have a conversation with him for
so long I had begun to forget. But between the pages was his
essence. Like a jigsaw, all the pieces were there, and all I had
to do was to piece them together and a map emerged.

I am acutely aware that my account has him coming in
and out like a codicil, but he comes in and out of these pages
as he came in and out of my life. I don't want to embroider,
I want to tell the truth, and the truth is that past seven years
old I hardly knew him. He was always in my thoughts, but
so rarely there in reality, and when he was, it was all so very
fleeting. I don't want him to be a shadowy figure. I want him
to read as clearly as anyone else, but the feel of his presence
is so much more visceral than his flesh and blood, yet so
much harder to describe. I loved him, that's all I knew. He
was, and is, in every part of me and, but for the constant ache
of missing him, I felt privileged. I had the knowledge that,
wherever he was, whether he knew me or he didn't, locked
inside of him was the deep love any father has for his

daughter, a thing so tangible and so real that neither illness nor death could ever diminish it.

The brain operation hadn't worked. In retrospect, it was now thought to have been a dreadful mistake all those years ago. Dad had gone downhill rapidly and was now unable to recognise any of us. Maeve continued her every-other-day visiting, and I still went when I felt strong enough. When I did, I could shut my eyes and hold him close, inhale, and there he was, the strong man who'd held me as a little girl. The man described so succinctly in the *National Dictionary of Biography* as 'Tall, thin, dark and haggard, gentle, gracious, unworldly and unpractical'. Once, when I took my long-haired boyfriend, Gerry, with me on a visit to the Priory, my father stared at me blankly. I sat on his lap, my arms wrapped around his neck and attempted conversation; he didn't answer but, as we went to leave, he whispered to the space surrounding him, 'Robinson Crusoe'. Those were the last words I heard him say.

There had been unexplained bruising and Mum was sure that Dad was being hit. I saw the bruises, the pinch marks on his arms, the kick marks on his legs. It was denied, not looked into, palmed off as falls. He was trying to tell us something, impossible to understand, but the fear in his eye told us everything. I have a last image of Dad, walking unsteadily towards us along a polished floor, Mum rushing to reach him before he falls. We are strangers, but something tells him we are not going to hurt him. I block it from my mind, because rage would overpower me if I let myself think.

He had to be moved quickly. Preparations were made for him to leave the Priory, and go to somewhere safe, with people we could trust. James Gilmore, Maeve's eldest brother, a doctor married to a nurse, ran an old people's home in Abingdon. A quick-tempered, emotional, wildly affectionate man, he had been struck off the medical register for having an affair with a patient (whom he later married) and they ran their home with all the care and loving attention one could only dream of.

A few weeks later, on 17 November 1968, my father died. A cold turned into pneumonia and Mervyn, the youngest resident by thirty years, hadn't the strength to fight it. He was fifty-seven and I was nineteen.

I heard my bedroom door creaking open. It needed oiling; it always creaked. In my small dark room I felt a warm hand gently tapping on my arm. 'Daddy's gone, darling,' my mother whispered. 'It's all over for Daddy now.' She lay down beside me, we held each other softly and wept soundlessly. 'Go back to sleep, my love, there's nothing we can do tonight.' She walked out of the room and closed the door. I never saw her face. I went back to sleep because my father had died a lifetime ago.

On a freezing morning a week or so later we said goodbye for the last time. Four hundred people crammed into St James's Piccadilly to pay their respects to a man most hadn't seen for years. The rows of distinguished figures listened as John Clements read poems by Mervyn, and Tony Bridge, an old friend and Dean of Guildford, gave the tribute. He spoke of a uniquely talented man, a uniquely compassionate man. I walked through a sea of poets, writers, artists, actors and aristocrats and, as the cold Piccadilly air hit me, a weight lifted – at last we could begin to remember the happy times.

*

Shortly afterwards I went with Gerry to a cottage belonging to Biddy and Erasmus in Penryndaedrath, North Wales.

December 2nd 1968

My darling little girlie,

Please don't worry about me. I've had more love than most people ever dream of, and you three are my wonderful legacy. Daddy loved you very much – you have been a wonderful girl and I am proud of you. You have a strength and maturity and a great capacity for loving & Daddy would also have been proud of you. Try not to think of me as sad, I am proud to have been Daddy's wife, and nothing can last forever. The pain is over for him, and how can any of us be sad for that. What he has left in love and beauty is incalculable. It would be unnatural for me not to have a little pain, but all of us do. I love you all so much. Enjoy the beauty around you now and don't cry for me.

Looking back, it's hard to piece together what I was feeling at this time – sorrow, relief, a hundred cobbled-together emotions. I didn't fall to pieces, because I had known this day was coming for half of of my life. The lurking sadness began to dwindle, and I took succour in the freedom for his tormented mind that death would bring, and solace in the knowledge that his inner loneliness had at last ended.

After my father's death, life continued much as before, but there was a calm and a peace that I'd not known for a long time, and to see my mother released from her endless struggle was release for us all.

*

Maeve had begun writing *A World Away* while Mervyn was in the Priory. It was due to be published on general election day 1970, eighteen months after Dad died. She was fully prepared for snide reviews or, because of the election, no reviews at all but, instead, was stunned to receive generous and universally sympathetic notices from every paper. Anthony Burgess called it 'exquisite and poignant'; the *Financial Times* reviewer described it as 'unbearably moving'; the *Evening Standard* said, 'His widow has written no obligatory biography but a love story as strangely haunting as the talent of the man himself.' There was not a bad one among them, and we cried again, this time with happiness.

Proustian Lessons

We walked everywhere in those days. I didn't know anyone who owned a car, and waiting for a bus or a tube took too long, so Gerry and I would stride from Chelsea to the West End to see every new film in the opening week. Afterwards, we would wander through Soho to Jimmy's in Dean Street for a mouth-watering stew that fell off the bone, and finally a languorous wander through the park and home. They were translucent days. The atmosphere in London was brimming with optimism and days seemed to be got through without too much worry about the future. The future was far away and plans could wait.

After strolling from Sloane Square to the World's End, stopping every few minutes to say hello to a friend or acquaintance, the children of Chelsea parents congregated in the same place every Saturday morning. The children of aristocrats and of bankers, of artists and of mothers who lived above the shops, the children of World's End boys, all spent hours over lukewarm cups of coffee in the Picasso on the King's Road, or Guys and Dolls on the opposite side of the road. The cafes were teeming with beautiful boys and girls as everyone table-hopped in search of the elusive address of the party rumoured to be taking place that night. From the Picasso we'd move on into the Pheasantry, now a Pizza Express but then magnificent artists' studios, where painters Timothy Whidbourne, Martin Sharp and Nigel Waymouth all had studios.

King's Road had few shops in those days but the ones there were, were original, one-off places where you could buy a dress no one else would have, and your boyfriend could order a bespoke suit in midnight blue velvet. It wasn't what it is now, a sort of dreary Oxford Street with endless franchised clothes shops, ordinary staff and formulaic coffee bars. The boys had Granny Takes a Trip, Hung On You and Dandy Fashions to buy their funky, romantic clothes, and I once spent a whole week's wages on a loud statement of a man's coat in orange and green checked Harris Tweed from Quorum, Ossie Clarke's shop. A beautiful crêpe de chine dress and an embroidered cardigan could be picked up for a reasonable price in the Chelsea Antique Market and there was never a chance that anyone else would be wearing it.

London was more segregated, everything happened in a much smaller radius, and friends were more localised. We went to Blaises, the Speakeasy and the Scotch of St James but more often we went to friends' houses. We walked from Lord North Street to North End Road, from Earl's Court to Olympia, and everywhere surrounding and in between. Parents were never there, so we sat cross-legged on expensive Persian rugs, smoking weed and listening to the blues, to bluegrass, to soul, to Hank Williams and Janis Ian, to The Rolling Stones, to Smokey Robinson and The Lovin' Spoonful, to Love, Carole King, and The Holy Modal

Rounders, to Blood, Sweat and Tears, to Randy Newman and The Impressions, to Lenny Bruce and the Byrds and, of course, to Bob Dylan. Since his first album, every subsequent one was cause for celebration.

Sunday afternoons were spent listening to the eccentrics at Speaker's Corner, swimming and boating in the Serpentine, and lying on the grass in Hyde Park, enjoying the free concerts from The Rolling Stones, John Sebastian and The Who, amongst others. Money didn't come into the equation; people didn't talk about it or think about it, or the people I knew didn't. Our wages paid for rent, the cinema, the theatre, cigarettes, a new book and a new record once a week. What more could you want?

My friend Nonie had secured me a job at the Hungry Horse restaurant in the Fulham Road, where I sat in a little cubby-hole taking reservations and doing the bills, while the stream of glamorous regulars, including Francis Bacon, would take a stab at eating the delicious home-made pies. After work we would walk to Nonie's flat, where her boyfriend, the tailor Nigel Hayter-Preston, would be sitting cross-legged on the floor, pins in his mouth, shears in his hands, creating something exquisite from suede or leather. Oh how beautiful was the reversible black suede jacket with brown leather lining he made for me, and the cream suede coat with drop belt he made for Maeve.

Gerry and I read like people possessed. When I first met him, he had read two books, *What Makes Sammy Run* and *Absolute Beginners*, and for his birthday I bought him ten more – ten seminal books that would, if I'd got it right, point him in the right direction. From that day on he never looked back. We sat side by side in my mother's sitting room, with the bar heater full on, quietly reading to ourselves or

206

reading to each other. We devoured everything we could lay our hands on. We bought paperbacks from W. H. Smith in Sloane Square and we ransacked Maeve's book-shelves. We read Baudelaire and Rimbaud, Verlaine and P. G. Woodhouse, Nathaniel West, Graham Greene and Evelyn Waugh, Nancy Mitford, Rosamund Lehmann and Elizabeth Bowen, Keats, Raymond Chandler and Dashiell Hammett, Jerome K. Jerome, Patrick White and Basil Bunting, Wilkie Collins, Maupassant and Gunter Grass, L. P. Hartley, e. e. cummings and Patrick Hamilton, Henry Greene, Djuna Barnes and Dorothy Parker, Walt Whitman, Ronald Firbank and Robert Frost, Flaubert, Carson McCullers and Anthony Powell, Huysmans, Eudora Welty and Christopher Isherwood, James Purdy, Conan Doyle and Hardy, Balzac, John Cowper Powys and Edith Wharton, on and on and on. We couldn't stop. We were novices to literary criticism. Nothing had been ruined by being taught or dissected. We were just hungry, passionate and intoxicated, and all we cared about was the utter joy with which these books infused our souls.

Loving the huge novel, and loving the huge novel with a sequel even more, I was nervously looking forward to beginning Proust. I liked the idea that the next six to nine months were accounted for, stretched in front of me, taken care of, but I worried that I might find the books too difficult. Instead, I found that, like Dickens or the Russians, they were straightforward and completely readable. I adored the closeted world I settled into, loved the slowness of the pace, when a character entering an anteroom could take three pages until he finally opened the door and walked in. Those twelve volumes told me more about human nature than any other books I'd ever read. I decided that, if I were ever asked by a Martian to describe a human being to them, I would suggest that they read *À la Recherche du Temps Perdu* because everything they could possibly want to know about society and class, love and loss, jealousy and manners, etiquette and attraction was there.

Never again, I promised myself, would I question why so and so was with so and so. It took Proust to explain that there *was* no explanation. People fell in love with whom they fell in love with, and there was no point in trying to work out why. If you could be bothered to look, it usually became clear in the end. He might be an unprepossessing-looking chap, but he was witty and strangely sexy, and she might not be as exciting as you might have hoped for your friend, but she was warm and she laughed at his jokes.

London Air

Heroin addiction had reached epidemic proportions in the particular area of London where I lived, and it would have been very hard not to come across people who took it regularly. A touching friendship had been struck between Maeve and the boy who lived across the road, a sweet-faced, intelligent boy, recently expelled from Eton, a boy with an all-consuming habit. His father had died and his mother was left unable to cope with the sadness of watching her son crumble before her eyes; to escape the frequent and blazing rows, he would pop across the road, where I would sometimes find him and Maeve sitting together in the kitchen. One night, after he had left home to live with his girlfriend, he nodded off, leaving his cigarette to burn, and a fire started. He was badly burned. I went with Maeve to visit him at the burns hospital in Wimbledon, where they held hands, and I sat silently, moved by the quiet and tender friendship that had skipped the generations and arrived in a place that was safe, private and full of unspoken propinquity.

Every day there was another story – someone had jumped out of a tree and broken his neck, another had overdosed.

These were invariably nice people, handsome, intelligent and good company, a great number of them the people who made Chelsea the place it was, and I liked them very much, as did Maeve. I knew she was concerned for me. I understood her concern, but I was never tempted, and in the one full and comprehensive conversation that we had on the subject, I managed to convince her of my lack of whole-hearted commitment to anything other than weed. My own boyfriend was slowly recovering from a prolonged addiction, and many a month was spent in my kitchen, him too frightened to set foot outside and me trying to help him find a balance between paranoia and manic gregariousness. He was then living in a flat in the area they now call Brompton Cross, taking guitar lessons from Eric Clapton on the Martin guitar he had bought from Clapton with the proceeds of a £1,000 Premium Bond win. Painful hours were spent in my kitchen practising his E chords but something told me that Gerry was never going to be a rock giant.

Gerry shared the flat with David Litvinoff, a man in his late thirties. David had the quickest wit and the sharpest tongue of anyone I had ever met. He spoke at an extraordinary speed, his repartee skipping from one subject to another with the speed of a jaguar. It could be some juicy gossip of the day, an obscure Nietzsche quote, an unrecorded Mississippi Delta singer once heard and never forgotten, or the less obscure hierarchy of the English nobility. In other words, he knew a lot. He could be terrifying if he didn't like you, and there was no one whose Achilles' heel he couldn't locate in an instant. I saw confident men cut to shreds within a second by a sentence from David, and it wasn't a pretty sight. Luckily for me, I was never on the receiving end.

He was the most hilarious person I had ever met, and his observations might make any comedian of the past thirty years feel shy of calling themselves by that name. He had no possessions at all except for a bicycle and a reel-to-reel tape recorder that played a constant stream of Bessie Smith or Ma Rainey at full volume. In his empty room, he would dance wildly, his wiry, athletic body gyrating, his arms moving as swiftly as a flamenco dancer's, until porters and furious tenants rapped on walls or gave him ultimatums. He, Gerry and I spent endless days and nights together, talking and laughing until our stomachs ached. He was dialogue coach and part scriptwriter of *Performance* and would discuss with us the intricacies of making the film. They were having trouble with the title. Ideas were bandied about until eventually they decided to settle on *The Performers*, but still David felt that wasn't quite right. I suggested, instead of *Performers* what about *Performance*, and he liked that idea.

The first time we met I was invited to join him at a dinner party being given by some new friends of his. The hosts were two spinster sisters of over eighty. They were Janeites, Jane Austen aficionados. The cheery old ladies scuttled around the room, giggling and clutching their individual tin openers, which they brandished with all the pride of a Samurai warrior clutching his sword. Pilchards served straight from the tin were carefully placed on our plates, arranged as if this were a gourmet meal they had been preparing for hours. For pudding, we each had a cornet with a scoop of strawberry ice cream and an artistically placed chocolate flake poking out at a slant.

The dinner was spent in mad conversation that went to and fro between the sisters, David and John Crittle, a tailor who owned Dandy Fashions. Gerry contributed a spattering,

211

and, from me, utter petrified silence. The banter that went back and forth was abstruse and disjointed. Nobody's answers bore any resemblance to the question, but everybody nodded sagely as if they did. Although I had never been subjected to much in the way of ordinariness, this evening won first prize for the most peculiar dinner party I had ever been to. It was just another night in sixties London, where you could find yourself sitting next to anyone, gangster, poet, tramp – or Janeite.

Good Luck   Have a great time
Dear Clare and Gerry,
    Thanks a lot for your letter, which I got this morning only. The mail is apparently very delayed or something. I tried to ring you both a few minutes ago, but could not give the name of the subscriber, only the address, which was insufficient they said. Ah well. I am glad that after the long haul down (or is it up?) you are both digging the local scene(ery). Oh, I envy you country dwellers.
    Gerry said that you were fantastically isolated, that's me and 53 the buildings. Just now Mr Fraser, Mr Gibbs, Mr Richards and Miss Faithfull were here on Saturday night/Sunday morning, and as a result of some peculiar lie, an enormously unpleasant situation has arisen, devolving around a story which is obviously going the rounds in these ere parts. Hateful and strange.
    The film drags wearily and hysterically on. I am working a lot with James Fox at his and this place, and though he's very charming, once we get down to the real grass roots of the character he's to play, and the frightening areas of the psychotic, he gets very uneasy. I tell him that Devlin would almost certainly have used

a razor and dagger on his victims when he was younger, and describing the intrinsics of where this is at frightens and nauseates James, so there is a distinct air of chimera on the 'authenticity' of this xxx picture.

It must be very beautiful where you are, why not ring me up, or let me have your number and I'll ring you instead. How are you managing for bread?

Well my dears, all that you wish yourselves I hope it comes true. In the meanwhile, thanks for the letters, apologies for this drivel, write again soon, and love and kisses etc.

    x David x

Be cool   Relax and enjoy

David had hired a cottage in Kent so that he could write in peace, away from the hubbub in London, and I was invited to stay:

Givemeland 346   Go-To-Bed
                                          Gogoland
                                   Sunnymorningtime

Darling Clare

Christmas cards normally suffer an ignominious fate with me, but I feel about yours that this is something rather special. Your Father's drawing (Eve and the Serpent yes?) is so beautiful I shall try to keep the mantelpiece clean and tidy, to be worthy of the card. My fondest love to you and yours.

Gerry says he'll be coming down here in early January. Excellent, but so much better if you can sneak off with him. We could all have such a groovy time. I wrote to him, with a 'potty' enclosure. Hope he got the

213

note. He sends me such funny letters, full of info, tempo and bel canto glissando down to his Celtic limbo. Oh! Oh!

I'll be in London over Christmas. I'll probably stay until the New Year, forward into the seventies with Harry Boy Wilson (Ugh!). My number will be Underhill 3310. Can we three meet and eat some meat and wheat?

Again, dear Clare, all my love to you and Gerry G.

Tell him I dug him etcetera on the cassette. It was too much. I can see great things ahead for him if he and J.I.G. should ever do a tour of the halls in the Midlands. G would be the straight man, and J.I.G could handle the patter-man's gig. There is no news from here. None at all. Tell Gerry I've had news from Keith Richards.

And Denis Deegan (a joint backstage p.c. from shrine auditorium San Francisco no less).

And from Jimmy Fox, who sends his love to Gerry.

Until we meet again.

David

P.S. Get Penguin Collected Short Stories Vol.2. It has a lot of my brother Manny's stuff in it.

I went to stay. It was bitterly cold and central heating was still a luxury in those days, a luxury noticeably absent from this small corner of Kent. Every morning we got up early, donned a motley collection of coats and hats and went in search of logs. We taught ourselves how to make roaring fires, which we sat around for most of the day, putting the world to rights and reading our books. One afternoon, in an attempt at all-over warmth, I decided on a hot bath. As I lay dreamily, soaking in the bubbles, I felt a shadow blocking out the winter sun. I looked up to see David standing on a ladder that was propped up against the bathroom window. He was waving at me. I waved back, he retreated down the ladder and it was never mentioned again. David was gay and I was puzzled as to why he wanted a look – perhaps it was just a question of aesthetics.

One day I was asked to make lunch for a large group of male friends of his who were coming to stay. Never having cooked a proper meal before, I succeeded, through adrenalin and sheer terror, in cooking a roast that has never been bettered, little knowing just how ahead of my time I was in placing the lamb and all the vegetables together in one tin and slowly roasting them all to perfection. After a brief introduction, one of these men, a black American called the Back-Breaker (not for nothing I soon discovered) hauled each one of us over his back like a sack of coal and then shook us roughly until we fell to the floor like depleted balloons, our heads spinning, our bodies shaking and our senses numbed by the shock. Still in a state of acute dizziness, he had another treat in store – just for me, the only girl in a house full of men. Placing me gently on a minute velvet foot-stool, he recited 'Willie the Shake', a Lord Buckley poem, an inch from my face, stared deep into my eyes and awaited my reaction.

I don't remember much more of that holiday, apart from listening to an acetate of *The Basement Tapes* for the first time. Eric Clapton had given it to David and David made me a copy. It would be seven years before *The Basement Tapes* was released. David rummaged his long fingers through a tapestry bag and pulled out the five LPs he had brought with him and we listened to *Highway 61 Revisited*, *Blonde on Blonde*, *Bringing It All Back Home*, Randy Newman's first album, *Randy Newman*, and *The Last Poets* from beginning to

215

end, day in, day out for a week. Bob Dylan was so influential in all our lives that when I think of myself post-thirteen, I realize that every record he released formed a backdrop for most of my experiences.

I was working at the American Express offices in the Haymarket when we heard that he was to play the Isle of Wight Festival on August bank holiday 1969. This was a massive coup – he hadn't played in England for three years. Gerry and I managed to get hold of some tickets and I hastily gave in my notice. We set off on our journey wittily singing 'We've Got a Ticket to Ryde', and showing off to hapless tube travellers on their way to work. We must have taken sleeping bags but I don't remember doing so. My overall impression of the whole experience was that long walk to find lavatories. I remember prolonged farewells, tripping over naked, face-painted mothers with their babies, dangling flowers wilting on improvised headbands, and meeting amid the hundred and fifty thousand every friend we'd ever known in our lives, peering bleary-eyed from a sea of beige tents.

When we finally found some relative comfort in a spot we could call home, our legs crushed to our chins, people sharing joints and freaking out on acid, we floated away to the music supplied by The Band, Richie Havens, The Who and many others. We were about five miles from the stage, but close enough to hear the man introducing The Band saying to Robbie Robertson, 'Hello, mate, before you begin I'd like to introduce all you people to a very special lady, my old lady, Julie Felix. And one more thing, people, I beg you, DO NOT take the brown acid!'

David was on a boat with Keith Richards and other pop luminaries and he invited us, but Gerry said, 'No thanks, we'd rather be on a muddy, smelly field, crushed, and miles from the action than sipping champagne with the nobs.' Queuing for hours for fish and chips and sloppy curry at two-and-six a throw, stretchers battled their way through the masses, while the crowd waited impatiently until 11 p.m. the following night for Bob Dylan to appear. When he finally did, dressed from head to toe in cream, the empty beer cans ceased their journey from field to stage as a hush descended on the restless crowd. 'Do you want the old songs or the new ones?' he called out. 'The old ones,' we screamed in reply. 'I'll do the new ones then,' he said.

An hour later when his set was finished, the hungry crowd bayed for more. Ricki Farr, the compère, tried his best to placate the audience. 'Bob Dylan came here to do what he had to do and he's done it, and I'm afraid that's the end' – a more succinct but less flattering message than his earlier, 'You are the blessed generation. You are the body beautiful. Thank you, keep it that way.' The following morning these two blessed body beautifuls joined the exodus from the now cheerless field, past the bewildered residents of the Isle of Wight, to queue for the ferry that would take them away from the best weekend of their lives.

A Cure in Ireland

I was never out of work. I took anything I could, and always enjoyed the experience, but I had a dream – a fervent but modest dream – and that was to work in the literature department of Dillons university bookshop in Malet Street, at the time the most important large bookshop in London. I rang weekly, but there was never a vacancy. I longed for this job like I'd longed for no other and so I persevered, and one day, just to be shot of me, I was given a date for an interview. I knew it would be difficult, with my non-existent exam results, to convince the manager to employ me in a shop where academics came to buy their books. At the end of a very pleasant interview I was offered a job, not in the literature department, but in goods inwards, where I would unpack books until someone decided to leave.

Goods inwards was far more fun than I had expected it to be, and it was a very sad day when a position in hardback literature eventually became vacant. People came in and out all day long to chat as I unpacked the books, and we danced to the music playing on my portable radio tuned in to Radio Caroline. On the shop floor I quickly noticed the difference between the assistants in the various departments and, without wanting to stereotype too much, the people in Education, Travel and Politics were a far more serious bunch than, say, Literature, Poetry, Paperback Fiction or Penguin up on the mezzanine where you could discuss 'The Nibelungenlied' and your lipstick tone and enjoy both discussions equally.

This was in the days of Laura Ashley dresses down to the ground and the natural look, which I've never been a fan of, much preferring the unnatural look and dyed blonde hair over the real thing. Desperate affairs were going on behind every bookcase, so much so that we'd get extremely irritated by the customers and their constant nagging for books. When we tired of kissing each other, we'd play Botticelli and mull over the question while pondering the intricacies of shipping thirty-five novels to Dubrovnik. We all had crushes on each other. I had an enormous crush on a boy in Paper-back Fiction, mainly fuelled by his gentle and thorough explanation of 'To His Coy Mistress'.

Early one morning, alone in my section, as I unpacked new books and dusted shelves in preparation for the slow but constant trickle of professors, browsers and new students of literature, I spotted a lone woman. She was pulling out books from the G–H section and I vaguely wondered what she was looking for. From her old-fashioned clothes and peppery bun, I unfairly discounted her as either a Hesse or a Gide buyer, but she didn't look quite Galsworthy either. I was idly passing the time when my eyes wandered down her shapeless dress and landed on her legs. Bulbous purple stripes, which at first I took for perplexingly modern tights, caught my eye, and I suddenly realised with horror that these were varicose veins. I can hardly write the words without feeling faint, let alone have them so proudly on display. The prickly sensation began under my arms, and then it began. I could feel myself begin to swoon, but somehow I managed to crawl past this completely oblivious woman and into the tiny stock room, where I had a full-blown faint. I came round with my head placed on someone's lap and a cold cloth pressed to my forehead as I took small sips from the obligatory glass of water. Unable to tell anyone what had happened (in case I fainted again), and making sure the woman had left, I returned to the world of hardback literature, helping the new girl with the authors she hadn't heard of and trying to get her out of the habit of sending people to the wrong department for the books they were after. 'Try the medical department,' a poor customer was brusquely ordered when enquiring after Gwen Raverat's *Period Piece*.

I tended not to let anyone know I was Mervyn's daughter and it took a while before it was discovered at Dillons. The reason I never said wasn't disingenuous, but it was self-preserving. Occasionally, people liked to give me their opinion of his work, letting me know where he'd gone wrong, and the authors they did have time for. It was unfair of me, though. I should have known that this was unlikely to happen at Dillons, because it had never happened at any of the other bookshops I'd worked in. It was in the outside world where the same stale sentences came out of the same stale mouths. 'I found them impossible to read,' little pause, coy smile, 'I've tried.' Or 'No,' big pause, shake of head, honest, emphatic opinion, 'I didn't like them at all.' And the hardy perennial, 'Was he on drugs?'

I was never sure what I was supposed to do with these comments – argue his case, nod in agreement or sympathise with the time they had wasted – so I just stood rooted to the spot as their superior opinions left me speechless. I am more sanguine now, and let them have their moment, if it makes them feel better, but when I was young I wanted to find a corner to curl up and die in, or better still, aim a perfect punch at their sneering faces. I wanted to say, 'I wouldn't stand there criticising your father's work, so don't criticise mine,' but of course I didn't, because it wasn't the same thing and I knew it. However unrealistic it might have been, I found it impossible to be hardened to a certain sort of smug criticism. I wanted to protect him, and his work, from the clever remark.

My time working in bookshops had come to an end and London was emptying fast. My long-term friends were all travelling in the East, bumping into each other round the side of a temple in Afghanistan with as much ease as if they were having a chinwag on Fawcett Street. While my soul was still satisfied with London and what I knew, I realised with a tremor of failure that I wasn't and never would be an adventurer. People seemed changed when they returned; whether it was drugs or whether it was a spiritual awakening is hard to say.

My relationship with Gerry was over. I had fallen in love with someone else. But I still missed him terribly, and was desperately sad at the end of the friendship that would naturally cease with the end of our relationship and the beginning of another one. I decided to go away and think about things, and meet my new boyfriend in Dublin a few weeks later when I felt more in control. I arranged to stay with my mother's elder brother, Roderick, and his wife, Grace, at their farmhouse in Castelwellan, County Down. I hardly knew them, but I knew that Ruth, Maeve's sister, was also staying. The prescription worked – the break from London did everything it was supposed to do. As the four of us sat in the sitting room every evening after supper, I slowly began to feel better. Getting to know my family did the trick in all kinds of ways. Ruth taught me to crochet, Roderick taught me to drive, Grace taught me to make pastry and all three got me hooked on *The Archers*.

While I was there, Mum wrote to me frequently.

My Darlingest girlie

Your letter arrived this morning and I was so pleased to receive it. It must seem strange to be where you are. It's the Mountains of Mourn, not Morn, which somehow seems more beautiful in a way.

I expect by now you will be getting a feel of the place and I hope you won't be homesick at all, at all!

Darling, I know things have been very difficult for you, and you haven't been any trouble, it's only that I hate to see you unhappy. I want to see you gloriously serene, and I hope perhaps the get away, into somewhere quite different, may help you to reach some kind of equipoise. I'm sure you are being a great success there. If you want to write something, why not simply make notes of things you see, or hear, or think, so that in time, when you really want to write, you can call upon such observations, as only too soon, impressions fade, never to be recaptured.

Dillons had a bad fire, the record department quite destroyed and the political department. It was the wiring apparently. Literature was alright.

I am going to the Paris Pullman next week to see a Russian film of The Cherry Orchard, which is apparently very good, and I want to go to see a film in Holborn, the something or other of the bourgeoisie. I'm reading Stevenson and I think he's a wonderful author. I think Dad was rather influenced by him, both in the style of writing and his content; although very different, one can sense the mood that is so much part of Dad's writing.

I am going to the BBC on Wednesday, to a rehearsal of the Flying Bomb. I hope there won't be any about!

Darling I love you very much – I am so glad that you are my daughter, and I want you to be happy.

All my special love to you, and love to everyone from me.

From your always loving
Mum

X   X   X

My Darlingest Clarie

Thank you so much for your two loving, funny, interesting and informative letters. I haven't rung because I thought it might be difficult for you to talk, but I'll ring you on Wednesday evening.

I'm so terribly glad that you are happy there and that they are all so kind to you. I had quite a funny letter from Auntie Ruth. Now that she's getting to know you, she's becoming very fond of you. I think it's really that you've always refused invitations that she hasn't got to know you before.

I miss you very, very much, but I'm certain that the break was inevitable, and somehow, seeing and hearing and thinking new things is so good – otherwise one gets into a tiny little world and can only see one side.

It's awfully good about the provisional driving licence, so funny, too.

The scaffolding is being put up – real hunky men, I don't see them joining a poetry reading circle! I don't know how long it's all going to take, but there's a great deal of tea-making throughout the day.

Sebby and Fay both ask a great deal about you. We all want to see you happy – as you should be. I'm so glad I've got a little daughter.

I'm going up to the BBC tomorrow for a rehearsal of the Flying Bomb and going to see *The Seagull* today.

I'll write again soon darling and phone you tomorrow evening.

All my special love
from your loving Mum

My Darling Clarey,

It was lovely talking to you last night – and I do hope that you are still having a good break. At least it's a new experience.

I hope you will be able to get a bit of driving in. Couldn't you simply get a piece of cardboard and draw an L in lipstick, if there isn't any chalk about?

It was very interesting at the BBC yesterday. It's always strange to hear Dad's words being spoken and interpreted by people, and becoming part of a programme, in a studio dominated by incomprehensible computer machines, and remembering how they had been written in silence and great urgency. It's rather wonderful really, and I wish he could know about it.

Tristram Cary, who has done the music for it, has an idea of it being performed in a City of London church, but I'm not quite sure how the babe could be managed. I think it could be most wonderful. The wife of the man who reads the sailor is a niece of Dr Hewitt from Sark. Ah! It's a small world, it is indeed!

Darling, I hope that you are being able to think a little about everything. I know it has been a terribly difficult time for you, and I want to see you having a life that is good and satisfying.

You are my darling daughter, and I shall always love you, but sometimes I think that too much may make it difficult for you to lead your own life. I hope not, though.

I have just had a nice letter from Auntie Grace, saying how well you have fitted in.

All my love darling

Your loving Mum

After a month or two I came home, refreshed, invigorated and on the look-out for work. Dillons had been a very happy experience, but I needed a change. I began working for Kate, Georgie's mother, in her flower shop in Cheval Place, Knightsbridge. My knowledge of flowers was rudimentary, to say the least, and now, with a heart full of shame, I wonder what the poor paying customers thought when they were delivered my cone-shaped floral offerings. Pat, a large red-headed woman, who also worked for Kate, knew an awful lot about flowers, and occasionally I accompanied her to the mini-gardens of Knightsbridge to seed and sow. But gardening was tinged with difficulty from the start on account of my worm phobia. Every time my spade unearthed one I screamed with revulsion, but Pat was extraordinarily patient under the circumstances and, over the summer, we perfected a method where I would hand her the tools, like a nurse to a surgeon, and keep my eyes shut if a wriggler should reveal itself.

I was much happier working in the shop, serving the rich and emaciated women of Knightsbridge. Ava Gardner was the highlight of my day. She strolled past the shop most afternoons, sometimes alone and sometimes with the actor Charles Grey, with whom I think she was staying. She always gave a little wave as she walked by and I would wave back at this still-beautiful woman as I wrapped up some love-in-the-mist, or, as Kate called it, fuck-in-the-fog.

One morning, walking down Montpelier Street on my way to work, I saw Rod Steiger coming towards me. This synchronicity, this serendipitous crossing of paths was truly astonishing because I had just been thinking of him. I had been to see *The Pawnbroker* only the night before and had been extremely moved by both the film and his unbearably harrowing performance. Seeing him in a depressing pawnbroker's shop in New York and a cobbled London street within twenty-four hours struck me as remarkable, so I waylaid him and told him of the coincidence. After I had congratulated him on his seminal piece of acting, he looked genuinely thrilled, kissed my hand and went on to say sweet things of a perfectly charming but less cerebral nature. His flirtatious grin and twinkling eyes were extremely provocative and, although I had never found older men attractive, I was surprised to find him and his short, sturdy body very sexy.

London was much emptier then and casual encounters with people you wanted to meet seemed easier. Popping out late one night for some New England ice cream, I had my second Beatles experience. A Rolls-Royce sidled up to the kerb just as Georgie and I were leaving the deli across the road from my house. John Lennon and Paul McCartney popped their heads through the wound-down, blackened-out windows. 'Hop in girls, fancy coming to a club?' they asked. My sluttish foot was halfway through the door when Georgie's voice reverberated behind. 'No thank you. C'mon Clare, let's go.' I edged the top half of my body back out of the car. 'No, I'm sorry. Thanks anyway,' I said as the lights turned green, and I watched in misery as they zoomed down the Old Brompton Road in search of girls with more on their minds than sitting in a kitchen with a tub of ice cream and two spoons, listening to The Beatles.

Maeve Discovers Britain

My brothers had left home long ago and I often had the house to myself. Maeve's life had become an incredibly full one – dinners here, dinners there, exhibition openings, painting, the cinema, and her weekly visiting, reading to and shopping for whichever elderly person she had been assigned to next. If and when they died, she would be assigned another one, but when Kensington and Chelsea council gave her an old woman who moaned incessantly and was rude to Maeve, I was furious. Mum laughed and said that to get angry rather defeated the object. To say, 'I just want a nice one please,' wasn't the point. No one apart from me knew about this other side of her life. She made nothing of it, but I expect after her experiences with Dad she knew just how valuable a regular visit from someone with a friendly face could be. So for a while we met like ships in the night.

She had a companion, of whom, over time, I became extremely fond. After my father died, and even before, she had men swarming round her like bees round a honeypot. Some I didn't like at all, others I did. With the writer John Watney, I felt secure in his affectionate and respectful treatment of my mother, and I never wanted her to be lonely.

Maeve had discovered late in life that she rather liked the country, and with a touching enthusiasm, she and John began taking frequent little jaunts into an undiscovered Britain.

Dorset

Here are some of the ponies we saw on the way down. It's so beautiful and remote. I ran into Jude yesterday! And Angel Clare, Clare Angel, Love Mummy.

Beckley Sussex

My Darling Clarie

We had a good journey down, and the cottage is everything one could wish for. Down a long lane, past the big house, and completely alone. It's marvellously equipped, with washing machines and telly (if you like that sort of thing!). At the moment it's pouring, though we are going to explore a little. The silence is wonderful. A small field mouse came to offer its hospitality last evening and this morning a herd of black and white cows made their placid, unhurried way past the cottage, stopping every now and then for no reason at all, except 'to stand and stare'.

Argyll

My darling Clarey

I'm writing this at 7 a.m. and watching out of the windows six horses and their foals eating grass which is as green as it used to be in 'England's green and pleasant land', and out of the mist appearing little islands that remind me of Sark. It is exquisitely beautiful and,

229

darling, I can't tell you how I sang for joy when I saw, felt and heard the rain.

The journey on the train was not quite the Orient Express but fun, and yesterday driving here was very quiet, alongside Loch Ness (whom I saw) but no one else did – not the monster, but a kind of mixture of a white horse and a tortoise. I am really enjoying it all and not thinking about anything (which you might say is not difficult for Mum).

from your loving Mum

Kiss Curl

My mother had cancer. Feeling perfectly fit, and enjoying life to the full, her children all married, her social life as buoyant as ever, she went to the doctor's to see about the arthritis in her hands, the one blot on her otherwise (for the first time) trouble-free landscape. The hereditary and painful arthritis that was now beginning to seriously hamper her knitting. She had appeared robust and healthy all her life, but the strain of keeping everything together for all those years had finally caught up with her. That day, Dr Roberts, twentieth cigarette burning away in his ashtray, suggested that since she was there, how about a once-over. 'Oh Maeve,' he sighed, after she had removed her top. 'Think we had better get you to the hospital.'

She had been making dolls for a while, Pierrots and Pierrettes, boys and girls knitted in mohair and silk jersey. The dandy men, with finger twiddling moustaches and lace ruffles around their necks, held hands with glamorous dancing girls dressed in full, multi-coloured dresses, who clasped bouquets of brightly coloured knitted flowers. Stuffed with laddered stockings, these boys and girls had no backbone and masses of them lay across bookshelves or sat hunched on radiators with their backs against the wall, often falling forward in a line, until straightened up again.

They lay along the skirting board of my bedroom, long since transformed into a playroom for Maeve's ten grandchildren.

I had been married to Charlie Penate for several years by now, and had two small children, Scarlett and Titus, and for a very brief time before Maeve became too ill, I used to take them to visit her every Wednesday afternoon. They adored playing in this room. Just like the kitchen, every inch was muralled. There were jungle scenes, and Arctic scenes and scenes from an English seaside. Crabs, shells, penguins, fish, seagulls, children, boats, donkeys and horses jostled for space with marmosets, lions, tigers, owls and birds of paradise. In 1981, they and this room were eventually incorporated into a children's book, *Captain Eustace and the Magic Room*, which she dedicated to her grandchildren.

Before becoming completely incapacitated, Maeve would paint all the time. In her tiny basement studio she put on her blue and white striped butcher's apron, rolled up the sleeves of her cream silk shirt and, with Radio 4 playing in the background, painted and drew her sad pictures. The stooped and naked figures of Mervyn were like a stark, progressive diary of a man in decline. La Famiglia restaurant was next door to the Langton Street Gallery in Chelsea, one of the two galleries that regularly showed her work, and we always went there to celebrate on opening nights. The pictures were sad, but she wasn't – she was happy and full of life.

It didn't take long, a couple of horrible years, with insufferable pain, and the same philosophical approach I'd become used to. She re-read the *Titus* books and she re-read

Proust. She'd read him every decade from the age of thirty and, nearing the end, she began again, but this time backwards and this time in French. She wanted to end, she told me, at the beginning. Nothing could compare to the beauty of reading them in the original, and to finish on the very first page took her back, reminded her of those happy days in Sark when we were small and life was just beginning.

I was baking a cake for my son Titus's third birthday party when the telephone rang. 'Please come,' my mother said. It didn't sound like her. Her voice was weak, but it was steely, and it came from another place, somewhere I'd never been before. She was far too ill to be making telephone calls and the knowing urgency frightened me. She'd never asked anything of me before and, as I made my way to the hospital, I knew she wanted to say goodbye, to look at us all one more time.

From all corners of London we raced to her, and found her coming in and out of consciousness, her laboured breathing desperate and scared. 'Please let me go,' she whispered as she attempted to pull the oxygen mask from her face. A priest was leaving the room as we arrived, had already given her the last rites. The room was packed with people and, for the least dramatic person I knew, it was the most dramatic of moments. Two of her sisters and two of her brothers were there. Her companion John Watney was there. My husband, Charlie, who was extremely close to Maeve, was inconsolable. My quietly weeping parents-in-law stood in the hall, looking after my perplexed children (Scarlett five and Titus three that day) who unknowingly had kissed their grandmother goodbye. But Fabian wasn't there. We hadn't been able to get hold of him until it was too late. I held my mother's hand and I kissed her and, in the early hours of 3

August 1983 she died, the kiss-curl she wore on her right cheek for as long as I could remember as pretty as ever.

The following morning, when Sebastian and I went back to the hospital to collect our mother's belongings, we bumped into the doctor who had been treating her. He told us her courage had been herculean, that her refusal to take morphine until the very end (she wanted her last days to be spent in consciousness with her family) resulted in the most agonising pain, which she attempted to camouflage when visitors came. Whenever I visited, pretty young nurses were always sitting on her bed, chatting to her, making her comfortable, sharing little jokes. Forgetting how easy it is to become extremely close to new people you see on a daily basis, I was ashamed to recognise a small twinge of jealousy when I saw how fond of each other Maeve and the nurses had become.

The doctor went on to say that, although he knew it wasn't the appropriate time or place to mention it, he felt he had to say something about her skin. The nurses had commented on the whiteness, the softness, the lack of lines. I thought it was a lovely and funny diversion from the sadness we were feeling, and told him so. I explained that she'd never liked the sun and sat under an umbrella in the summer. She'd visited a hot country just once in her life, and then couldn't wait to get home to the rain. And I said that underneath it all, Maeve was an Irish girl whose skin was, as a consequence, exactly as he described.

Desert Island Everything

I didn't cry at my father's funeral, and I couldn't cry at my mother's. 'Let go, Clare,' Phyllida, my sister-in-law and friend, urged me, but I couldn't, the tears just wouldn't come. I felt strangely immune. These two people I loved with all my heart were gone, but I didn't want to cry. My luck had been fathomless. How had I managed to have not just one but two people who gave me everything I could have ever wanted, except time? And I was free, an adult, able since childhood to stand on my own two feet, to love whom I wanted to love, and be whom I wanted to be.

After my parents died, there was a smell that clung to the few possessions they had, which brought them back to me with unimaginable force. Seventeen years after my mother died I opened the small suitcase she had taken into the Charing Cross Hospital for the last time. In it was a black, mock patent leather handbag with a huge white sticker plastered on the front, her name and the date of death typed in large capital letters. As I opened the clasp, the smell was overwhelming. She poured from the bag like a genie, gently teasing me – open it up, she's there, close it shut, she's gone. Disjointed words from conversations flew into the atmosphere like notes from an instrument. I closed the bag, then opened it again, and clasped a neatly starched white hankie to my nose, the vapours clinging to the cotton like a compressed recollection. I sat on a packing crate in my basement and wept as I brought out, one by one, the last things that she thought important enough to take into hospital for the final time. A tiny gold diary with hospital appointments marked with a vertical line, three letters all written on the same day, and arriving on the day she died, one from me, one from Phyllida and one from John Watney, a copy of William Trevor's new book, *Fools of Fortune*, photographs of her children, a pink lipstick, a powder compact, an eyebrow pencil, a packet of honey-coloured hairpins and a comb. That was it – all so ordinary, all so poignant, all infused with the uniqueness of anyone's mother. And my father, nearly forty years after his death, I can smell him, too, any time I want to. He clings to the books that belonged to him. It is universal, the same for everyone.

At the end of every school term my mother and I would go to Peter Jones for lunch. We would take the lift to the fourth floor and wait until we could find ourselves a window seat overlooking Sloane Square. My elation was palpable; no more nuns, no more getting into trouble, just freedom – marvellous freedom. What did we talk of then? School, I suppose, books, paintings, my father and brothers. There were girls at school with names she loved to hear. She would whisper them to herself as though it was the first time she'd heard them. 'Oh, what a wonderful name,' she'd say – Charmian Sadgrove, Lamorna Heath, Nenina Lee.

A month or so before she died, Maeve came out of hospital for a short break from her treatment. I'd gone to Peter Jones to do some shopping and was waiting, as always, for the lift that never came, when to my astonishment the doors opened to reveal a beautiful woman standing alone in the lift that was naturally going down when I was going up. It was Maeve. It was like greeting a friend incongruously and out of context. It took a while to register the face I knew so well, and we both laughed at the coincidence of timing. We rumbled slowly upwards to the fourth floor and had our final coffee and last glorious hour together in our favourite place, where we had been going since I was a baby. I was utterly aware of the finality of the meeting. She was, too, but neither of us alluded to anything other than that wonderful moment of serendipity. We looked down from our window table at the small figures running through puddles and queuing for taxis in the square, like we had so many times before. We talked of her grandchildren, who they were and who they'd become. We didn't acknowledge the pain she was suffering, not from bravery or cowardice, but because she wanted to forget and enjoy the short time we had together.

We talked of books and films and songs and artists that had made a difference to her life, playing our favourite game, Desert Island Everything, compiling our lists for the last time.

'Ultimate choice now, Mum. Favourite song?'

'Blue Moon.'

'Favourite painter?'

'Cezanne.'

'Favourite book?'

'*Wuthering Heights.*'

'Favourite film?'

'*Jules et Jim.*'

'I want more choices, darling,' she suddenly said. 'I want

La Strada, I want *A Day at the Races*, I want *Le Grand Meaulnes*, I want Picasso, I want sweet peas, I want Arpège, I want the most perfect cigar Cuba has to offer, I want Daddy's poetry, I want him.'

Arm in arm we walked out of Peter Jones and into the King's Road, down Blacklands Terrace and into her favourite shop in the world, John Sandoe's bookshop, where she had been going since it opened. She was eager to buy William Trevor's new book to take back to hospital. John Sandoe was there, and they talked together as they had talked so many times before, while I scanned the new books in the centre of the shop.

There was one more outing before she went into hospital for the last time. She rang and asked whether I could get a babysitter at short notice because she had a sudden yearning to visit the new Waterstone's bookshop in the Old Brompton Road. She wanted to see for herself a superstore bookshop, and it was only a short walk from home. I collected her from Drayton Gardens, and she held my arm tightly as we walked slowly down the Old Brompton Road. Halfway there she stopped and, in the middle of the pavement, wept for the first time in my presence. The pain was unbearable. I was terrified by this sudden sob of hopelessness that exploded from deep within her. 'I want my mother,' she whispered as she gripped me. We turned around and headed home.

I think about my parents a great deal now, and miss them in a way I didn't then, in a mature way, with no tears but with a raw disappointment at not having known them for longer. I long for my children to have known them, to have experienced their warmth, their charm, their imagination.

And for myself, I yearn to sit in a Soho pub talking to my

father over an unhurried drink. I want to ask him question after question, the biggest of things and the smallest of things. I want to hear his now-diminishing voice tell me his likes and dislikes. I want him to tell me about his friends, the artists and the poets who made the 1940s so unique. I want him to explain why he loved *The Magnificent Ambersons* even more than *Citizen Kane*, what it was that he had against tartan, why, of all the film stars he could have chosen, he found Barbara Stanwick so sexy, and why, when he bathed me, he always sang 'Bye Bye Blackbird' and then always cried.

I want to ask him what it was like to live in China as a boy and Dean Street as a young man. I want him to tell me what he felt when he first saw my mother. I want to ask him what it felt like to be able to write *and* draw with such brilliance, and whether he ever had a moment of immodesty, when he allowed himself a clap on the back for his extraordinary achievements. And because he hated and he loathed what he saw as his inability to provide for his family in the way he longed to, I want to tell him that there wasn't a single thing we needed that we weren't given.

But more than any of this, I want to tell him how proud I am to be his daughter. Then I want us to walk tipsily out of the dark, unfashionable pub, and into the sunlight, my arm linked through his, my head resting in the crook of his tall shoulder as we carry on our conversation.

Romance in the Dark

The extreme romanticism of my parents left an impression on me as indelible as a birth-mark, the significance of love, and it being the thing that ultimately mattered, was a constant thread. 'Everything needs love; nothing survives without it,' my mother had said. In the week she died, she said how lucky she'd been, how the pain was inconsequential in comparison to the love she had received all her life. 'How lucky I've been with my darling husband, my darling children,' she said. I disagreed. I told her she hadn't been lucky. She was loved by me because she knew how to love, how to leave me alone to be myself, how to step back and allow me to make my own mistakes without interference, how to love me tenderly and uncritically, and without any of the strings so often fastened on.

After she died, my brothers and I spent every Sunday going through our parents' lives in Drayton Gardens. Sorting through Maeve's dressing table, among the lipsticks, eyebrow pencils, scents and hankies, I found letters from the butcher, touching little notes scrawled on the backs of order forms that cleared up the mystery of why it was always me who had to queue for the lamb chops and not her. 'I simply never get served, darling,' was her curious response. 'Dear Mrs Peake, you are a beautiful woman. I think I have fallen in love with you,' said one note, and others repeated the same sort of thing. To go through someone's drawers is such an invasion of privacy; the ordinary belongings of a loved one suddenly become so important. The button to some unknown shirt, the half-used lipstick, the crinkled rose from some unknown occasion, all take on an out-of-proportion significance, and these private little notes from the butcher that she would never have been so disrespectful as to disclose to anyone made me weep.

Sebastian and Fabian were in Mervyn's studio sorting through the thousands of loose drawings when Fabian called up. 'Clare, there's a letter for you in Dad's drawer.' I raced downstairs. Written ten months before she went into hospital for the last time, it was unfinished.

Charing Cross Hospital
October 5th 1982

My dearest darling Clarey, You have been the most darling daughter that anyone could wish to have, and as you have grown your touch and understanding have grown immeasurably sensitive, and I think of you as my friend.

I want your life to be fulfilled. Think of me as I was in my best days. I love you all so much. The world is changing so rapidly, that it will be very unlike the one you grew up in, but I know you will have the wisdom to guide your own children.

I am leaving so much of Daddy's work unresolved, and it will be almost too much for you three to know what to do about . . .

241

There *was* so much of our father's work to go through. We began the arduous and emotionally draining task of dividing everything into three. It was done simply and with no fuss. Three similar-sized paintings would be leant against a wall, then three more, and we took it in turns to be the first to choose until all the paintings were done. Then we moved on to the drawings, then sketch pads, pipes, the piano, the wooden table, the easel, until the whole of Drayton Gardens was dismantled. The order we were met with made the task so much easier, but still the volume of work meant that it took every Sunday for months. Any painting or drawing by Mervyn or Maeve of one of us would automatically belong to that person, but aside from that, it was a very democratic affair. Then there were the books to divide, hundreds of wonderful books, signed affectionately, signed admiringly, to Mervyn from many of the literary giants of the twentieth century.

Having been left for so long while Maeve was in hospital, the house had become a lonely place. The smells of stews and roasts, the strains of Billie Holiday calling from the basement to the next four floors, the preparations for her thrilling parties, our kitchen dances to 'La Vie en Rose', the warmth of her greeting, the kisses she planted on the inside of the frosted glass that you kissed back, all escaped into the atmosphere. The backward kick my father did as he left the house, the echoing laughter of the two of them, just memories now. We thought about trying to keep the house, but couldn't, and shouldn't, and didn't want to try to recreate a time that had gone, a time that was simply what it was – a memory, our parents' lives and the lives that they created for us being from a world unrecognisable now. In any case, without Maeve and Mervyn it just became any old house, and none of us wanted to live with ghosts. The house was sold, the murals whitewashed as it became a home worthy of a lifestyle magazine, and as far removed from the unreconstructed house that the five of us had lived in as was possible to imagine.

So we packed the boots of our cars, drove to our separate houses, hung the pictures on our walls, put the books on our shelves, and got on with our lives, with a sense that it all hadn't lasted very long, that the ending had been premature. But my sorrow, and that is what it was, had a sweetness to it. I knew that what Mervyn and Maeve had given me I would carry with me always. They would forever be close, not so close as to give me claustrophobia, but just close enough that I could still breathe.